E-mails to a Young Seeker

E-mails to a Young Seeker

Exchanges in Mere Christianity

DAVID S. HOGSETTE

WIPF & STOCK · Eugene, Oregon

E-MAILS TO A YOUNG SEEKER
Exchanges in Mere Christianity

Copyright © 2011 David S. Hogsette. All rights reserved. Except for brief quotations in critical publications or reviews, no part of this book may be reproduced in any manner without prior written permission from the publisher. Write: Permissions, Wipf and Stock Publishers, 199 W. 8th Ave., Suite 3, Eugene, OR 97401.

Scripture quotations are from The Holy Bible, English Standard Version® (ESV®), copyright © 2001 by Crossway, a publishing ministry of Good News Publishers. Used by permission. All rights reserved.

Wipf & Stock
An Imprint of Wipf and Stock Publishers
199 W. 8th Ave., Suite 3
Eugene, OR 97401

www.wipfandstock.com

ISBN 13: 978-1-60899-549-3

Manufactured in the U.S.A.

To my loving parents, who constantly encouraged and loved me in the faith, even when I did not always share that faith.

Contents

Acknowledgments / ix
Introduction / 1

Exchange 1: Am I an Atheist or an Agnostic? / 10

Exchange 2: Why Do Theists Claim the Universe Had a Beginning? Isn't It Just as Reasonable to Hold to an Eternal Universe and to Believe That, Possibly, God Is the Universe? / 20

Exchange 3: Can't Some Things Be Created by Chance? / 28

Exchange 4: Isn't Evolution an Adequate Scientific Explanation for the Origins of Life? / 33

Exchange 5: But Isn't Theistic Creation Just a Mindless God-of-the-Gaps Idea? / 42

Exchange 6: I'm Having Some Problems Accepting the Cain Narrative in Genesis / 49

Exchange 7: Why Are There Genealogies in the Bible and Can They Be Used to Date the Earth? / 55

Exchange 8: Isn't the Bible Just a Bunch of Tales Compiled by Men to Achieve Their Subjective Agenda? / 62

Exchange 9: I Don't Know If I Can Trust the New Testament Record / 69

Exchange 10: Isn't It Irrational to Believe in Miracles These Days? / 78

Exchange 11: But, the Resurrection of Christ Is Just a Myth, Right? / 84

Exchange 12: The Reliability of the New Testament Makes Sense To Me, but Why Should We Trust the Reliability of the Old Testament? That Just Seems Too Far-Fetched / 94

Exchange 13: I'm Having a Difficult Time Understanding the Christian Notions of Sin and Salvation / 100

Exchange 14: What about Those Who Never Hear about Christ? / 115

Exchange 15: With All This Sin in the World Caused by Us, Does That Mean God Failed and Let His World Get Out of Control? / 122

Exchange 16: For Free Will to Be Actual, Isn't God Required to Be a Manipulative Tester of Wills? / 127

Exchange 17: Can You Explain Original Sin? Why Am I Responsible for Adam's Sin? And Why Was Jesus Sacrificed? / 135

Exchange 18: What's the Deal with the Trinity? It Seems Like a Total Contradiction to Me. / 142

Exchange 19: Why Did Christ Have to Die? / 149

Exchange 20: Can't I Just Understand God in My Own Way? / 157

Exchange 21: I Have So Much to Think About—What Do I Do Now? / 164

Bibliography / 169
Selected Apologetics Resource List / 171

Acknowledgments

I would like to thank Craig Kempf, Frank Todarello, and Vincent Todarello for peppering me with excellent questions for a year and a half, forcing me back to Scripture and to my small study/library in search of answers. Also, thank you for encouraging me to compile all of our exchanges into this book. I offer special thanks to my dear friend and former pastor Rick Crews for reviewing major portions of the manuscript and providing excellent feedback. Of course, I take full responsibility for the contents. Heartfelt thanks to Alyson Crews for feeding me and allowing me to be the new recipe guinea pig. She is cook extraordinaire, who should definitely have her own cooking show on the Food Network. I thank the Crews children for tolerating me during so many lunches and dinners and allowing me to be silly when needed. Thanks to Reine Bethany for her diligent copyediting and for helping me tighten up my language and argument in various places. I thank my parents for their loving-kindness and for demonstrating how to love the unlovely. Finally, I thank my Lord and Savior, Jesus Christ, for the grace, time, and provision to complete this book.

Introduction

ANOTHER APOLOGETICS BOOK?

Conduct a search on apologetics on Amazon.com, and you will find more than 100,000 books on the topic. The obvious question immediately comes to mind: why write another book on the topic? Fair question. Christian apologetics has been around in various forms ever since Christ's earthly ministry. The New Testament Gospels are full of apologetic information. The book of Acts, Paul's letters, and many other letters in the New Testament contain apologetics. The fathers of the early church, great Christian theologians throughout church history, and learned Christian philosophers writing and lecturing up until today have all presented various defenses of the Christian faith. There exist presuppositional apologetics, historical and archeological apologetics, cultural and anthropological apologetics, and many other forms and combinations of these forms. Do we really need another book on the topic?

The simple answer is yes! One reason why so many treatises, essays, articles, and books have been written on apologetics since the first century is that human history moves through different phases of thought. Each new generation, each new cultural shift, and each new emerging social movement bring unique questions and sincere challenges to the truth claims of Christ and historic Christianity. With each new paradigmatic challenge, God raises uniquely gifted people within these intellectual, historical, and cultural contexts to address these new questions. More significantly, God raises special individuals within families, groups of friends, schools, universities, governments, churches, and communities to address the new challenges within their local spheres of influence. While these devout individuals may be unnoticed in the annals of intellectual history, they are vitally important to those within their communities who are sincerely seeking meaningful, honest, and truthful answers to their questions. And, they are individually significant to the work of the kingdom, used by a sovereign God for his glory and for the ultimate good of those seeking him. For, in truth, it is he who seeks seekers, reaching them through the efforts of those called to present answers and defenses of the Christian faith. It is this smaller, local context that gave rise to this book, and my prayer is that others may identify with this context and benefit from the questions and answers presented.

Moreover, people do not encounter issues of faith or engage the various questions in quite the same way. Because the cast of people's minds and the focus of their hearts are different, so too must be the apologetic approach. Indeed, many of the questions are the same or related on a fundamental level, but the method of addressing the questions ought to be contingent upon the audience. When it comes to engaging the difficult challenges of the truth claims of Christ, one size does not fit all. Just as Christ addressed the person individually as much as he confronted the question, so too must the contemporary apologist be sensitive to the heart and mind of the person asking the question and provide an answer that the questioner can comprehend. This is not to say that the underlying truth being expressed is somehow different. Rather, we must realize that the unchanging truth can be explained in different ways, and it is the task of the apologist to understand the seeker and attempt to explain answers in ways that an individual person will understand.

This book grows out of that sensitivity to the seeker. The intention of the book is to demonstrate in practical ways how to get to the underlying issues at the heart of the seeker's question and then to devise clear ways of providing cogent answers. In the various exchanges (or chapters) of this book, the seeker asks follow-up questions, and I strive to zero in on core issues. Thus, sincere apologetics is dialogic in nature, an exchange between unique individuals. For this reason, there is a need for a variety of apologetic resources so that a greater number of people can find compelling answers to the same fundamental questions, answers that make sense to them but that still illuminate the core truth.

PURPOSES AND LIMITS OF APOLOGETICS

It will be helpful to provide a very brief discussion of apologetics, its main goals, and its reasonable limitations. Very basically, apologetics is the defense of the Christian faith. Christ made various claims about the nature of reality, humanity, and the human heart, as well as claims about the condition of humanity's relationship to God, the unique and exclusive resolution to humanity's condition, in addition to many other material and spiritual proclamations. The reasonable question of the sincere seeker and honest thinker is simply: Are these claims true? If not, what is the truth? If so, what am I to do with these claims? Apologetics aims to sort through these issues and questions that each generation raises, to present clear and meaningful answers to these questions, and to explain and defend the rational foundations to these answers.

The Bible calls all Christians to "regard Christ the Lord as holy, always being prepared to make a defense to anyone who asks you for the reason for the hope that is in you; yet do it with gentleness and respect, having a good conscience . . ." (1 Pet 3:15–16). This is an early, first-century call for apologetics. Generally speaking, then, apologetics reveals and clarifies the truth claims of Christ, reveals and analyzes false claims, and exposes and explains the truth. People want to know about such things as the origin of the universe and life itself, the meaning of life, and the purpose of existence, morality, salvation, and ultimate destiny. Apologetics offers ways to provide specific biblical answers to these questions and to other such questions about God, Christ, faith, and many other biblical teachings. Apologetics also attempts to remove various intellectual, historical, cultural, and personal obstacles that block people from seeing Christ accurately, and that keep them from seeing clearly Christ's redemptive work on the cross. And, apologetics seeks to present coherent explanations of the truth of Christ and his teachings. This purpose is particularly important for our contemporary age in which coherence is dismissed as a constructed fantasy. However, incoherence is unlivable and rationally untenable, and deep down, when anyone asks a sincere, coherent question, that person is not satisfied with obscure, incoherent answers. Asking a question presumes the desire for, as well as the reality of, rational coherence. Many people have heard various contradictory claims about Christ, and Christian apologetics works through the contradictions to present coherent truth. This book explores a series of twenty-one tough questions asked by real seekers (more on that in a moment), attempting to present honest, factual, historical, scientific, biblical, and coherent answers to these important questions.

Yet, let me be clear. Apologetics has its limitations. I am not claiming that anyone can come to faith in Christ simply by having all of his/her questions coherently answered. As anyone who has watched debates between Christian theists and secular atheists knows, at the end of the day, sound arguments and overwhelming evidence can only, at best, win a debate. This victory does not guarantee the skeptic will suddenly believe. Scripture teaches that lack of faith is a condition of morality, of the heart, and of the will, not a matter simply of the intellect. As I reveal throughout the discussions in this book, Christian faith is indeed a reasonable faith, grounded in logic and evidence. However, true, deep, and abiding faith is ultimately a gift of God, a work of his Holy Spirit upon the heart, mind, and will of an individual. Yet, this gift is one that involves reason. God created us in his image, with capacities of reason and faith. It is important to emphasize that everyone operates by faith and reason. Strident atheists have faith that their logical arguments and conclusions correspond to reality (even as they may deny the existence of reality or the ability to know reality), just as Christian theists rely on faculties of reason and faith in sustaining their arguments for believing in Christ. The question becomes, who is right? We must deal on the level of ideas, on the plane of rational thought, but leave the ultimate transformation of will, heart, and mind to the Holy Spirit.

MY OWN JOURNEY

Speaking of such comprehensive personal transformations, it may be instructive to provide a brief survey of my own evolution, revolution, and conversion of mind, heart, and will. I was raised in a Christian home, and my parents were loving, God-fearing people who took me to church on Sunday mornings, Sunday evenings, and Wednesday evenings. My parents and the various churches I attended during the early years of my life taught me quite a bit about the Bible, God, Jesus, and salvation. I knew a lot of information, but I was rarely taught *why* I should believe this information. I was told *that* the Bible was true, but I was not instructed on *why* it was true. I was taught the claims of Christ, but I was never taught *why* they were true or *why* I should believe the Bible and the claims of Christ over the teachings and claims of any other sacred text or religious figure.

As a rebellious teenager, I began to question and doubt what I was taught, and when I went off to college and then to graduate school, my doubts transformed into skepticism, which then degraded into unbelief. What was the problem? My belief was *prescribed* for me; it was not really *explained* to me. I was thus an easy target for the skeptic. Ultimately, the skeptics kept me so busy questioning the claims of Christ that I never thought to question the claims of the skeptics. It never occurred to me to be skeptical of skepticism. Thankfully, my skepticism was later questioned and challenged by knowledgeable Christians. The more questions I posed, thinking I would debunk the claims and prove my own superior intelligence, the more answers were given and the more questions were asked of me. Suddenly, the stony wall of my doubt began to crack, and my mind was opened to facts and truths I had never heard before nor thought to consider.

Basically, I was accusing the Christian of being closed-minded without realizing the narrowness and closed nature of my own skeptical thinking. Recognizing my own hypocrisy encouraged me to explore the claims of historical Christianity with an open mind. I realized that my skepticism was itself a bias. It finally dawned on me that if I were honest with myself, my skepticism was blinding me and not allowing me to be neutral. I was not openly and honestly investigating the data. Once the veil of my own bias was torn, I began a journey of mind, heart, and spirit. In various ways, I felt both cheated by the church and deceived by the skeptics. I wasn't introduced to the core issues of the debate, if you will, and how both sides addressed them. So, I became familiar with the objections raised by such skeptics as Bertrand Russell, Anthony Flew (who, by the way, has experienced his own change of heart and mind upon further contemplation of the evidence), Peter Atkins, and Kai Nielsen. I analyzed their positions in relation to responses given by such Christian apologists as Ravi Zacharias, William Lane Craig, Norman Geisler, Peter Kreeft, and Alvin Plantinga. I also began reading works by such Christian thinkers as G. K. Chesterton, C. S. Lewis, R. C. Sproul, Os Guinness, Dallas Willard, and Paul Copan. Ultimately, this intellectual quest and spiritual journey in which I tested the claims of the skeptic and the Christian led me back to Christ and the historic claims of Christianity, such that now I not only know *what* I believe, I also know *why* I believe it.

This experience was not as simple and straightforward as my narrative account suggests. It was a fierce internal battle. At times I felt totally lost, other times angry, and many times confused. I felt like one of Socrates' cave dwellers discovering a whole new reality that turned my own upside down. What I eventually realized was that the Holy Spirit was actually turning my world right side up. My point here is that a true and abiding faith in Christ is not a mindless endeavor, it is not a mere crutch for the uninformed, and it is not for the weak at heart. The believer is often accused of holding to blind faith. Well, I discovered that my skepticism was far more blind than is my belief in Christ. To borrow a phrase that is the title to one of my favorite books, I do not have enough faith to be an atheist.

I should also note that my journey is not finished. I continue to learn and grow in faith, and this faith is dynamically experiential. I am blessed to be the faculty advisor for various Christian student groups on my campus where I teach literature and composition. I am further blessed to be engaged in Christian outreach in China, working on both the material level of providing love and care for poor and orphaned children as well as on the spiritual level of engaging Chinese college students in their own journeys of faith. These contexts present many unique challenges that test and strengthen my faith and encourage me to continue digging deeper into the heady matters of defending the faith and living it out. It is a daily walk in which the deeper joy that comes through triumphant successes and devastating failures, glorious happiness and deep sorrow, delightful pleasures and painful suffering are nearly inexpressible. There is a transcendent and eternal fulfillment to abiding faith in Christ that must be experienced to be understood.

ORIGINS OF THIS BOOK

I never set out to write an apologetics book. I have been so occupied with reading the work of key figures in the field and applying it to my own apologetic practice that it never really occurred to me to write such a book. Moreover, the idea to compile this book was not my own. So, how did this book come into being? Shortly after I began my study of the claims of Christ and the claims of Christ's critics, I became acquainted with a lively group of young professionals in their late twenties and early thirties. We became good friends and began e-mailing each other about all kinds of topics, from culture, to politics, to religion. For a brief period, we met at a local Starbucks once a week, and discussed varied ideas, opinions, and views, most of the time zeroing in on religious issues and matters of faith.

It is hard to characterize the religious views of this group (and this is an important lesson for anyone interested in engaging people via apologetics: do not put people in an ideational box, because that unfairly sets up delimiting expectations). However, if I were to describe them, it would be something like the following (and they agree with my descriptions here). All of them were theists to varying degrees, believing that an Intelligent Creator fashioned the universe and designed life, yet some were more agnostic than others on the details of this divine act of creation. It would be fair to say that their views ranged from deism to theism on specific issues as related to the created universe, the diversity of life, and the existence of intelligent life. Yet, they were also confused about terms such as *atheist, agnostic,* and *theist,* and we spent time discussing those categories. Some of these friends were raised in an explicitly Christian home and others not, and they ran the spectrum of agnosticism and skepticism on various teachings of the Bible and doctrines of historic Christianity. They were sincere seekers, coming to the discussions with minds open to various possibilities, lines of reasoning, and strands of evidence, and they definitely approached the discussions from a meaningful skepticism. In other words, their doubts and questions were not intended to bolster a hidden atheism; rather, they applied a rational skepticism in order to dig deeply into the issues and to discover truth. Although they may not have always agreed with me on various points, they were willing to engage the arguments and discuss the evidence as openly and honestly as they could. In this sense, they were sincere seekers.

Most of our interaction occurred online via e-mail exchanges. This group peppered me with many serious questions, challenging me to explain my biblical Christian theism and to provide evidence for my claims. We sustained this electronic dialog for a year and a half. This is an important point of the book: believers in Christ should prepare themselves and be willing to engage the sincere seeker for extended periods of time. Apologetic witnessing of this sort is deeply dialogic. When our discussions came to an end, these friends thanked me for dedicating the time to consider and address their many questions, and they expressed gratitude at how helpful it was for them personally as they continued to grapple with the issues. A few weeks later, they encouraged me to consider compiling our e-mail exchanges into a book. That thought had not occurred to me, and I wasn't convinced that such a task was feasible. With further encouragement and permission from these friends, I resolved to write this book.

I began reviewing the hundreds of e-mails that were written back and forth over that year-and-a-half period, and I was amazed at the volume and range of our discussions. How was I going to contain all of this material in the format of a book without losing the dynamic nature of the exchanges? I decided that the best approach would be to fashion a single composite young seeker who would give voice to the various questions. Since many of our discussions touched upon experiences some of my discussion friends had in college grappling with these issues, I decided to position this fictional young seeker as one of my university students. I am a professor of English language and literature at a technical university in New York, and I have had similar exchanges with some of my students outside of class (though not nearly to this extent or at this depth). I decided I could create this student voice with a fair degree of authenticity.

After sorting through the e-mail messages, I organized the content into twenty-one key questions that my friends raised. I arranged the questions in basically the same order in which they were asked, reordering only a few of them to lend a smoother logical flow to the book. In most cases, I have also maintained the back-and-forth exchanges on many of the questions. For this reason, I refer to the chapters as exchanges in order to illustrate the dialogic nature of the conversations. I also shared drafts of these exchanges with my dear friend, who was my pastor at the time I wrote the first draft of this book, and he provided many helpful suggestions for revising and clarifying various points. The final result is the book you hold in your hand.

HOPE AND PRAYER FOR THIS BOOK

I intend this book for two main audiences: (1) the sincere seeker struggling with questions of faith, and (2) the faithful Christian struggling with trying to explain and defend the claims of Christ. I say the following as sensitively and respectfully as I can: if you are a hardened skeptic or an entrenched atheist, then this book may not be for you. I would encourage you to give it a chance, but if you are not interested in an honest and open exploration of the arguments, then this book may not help you. It is my prayer, however, that you would soften your heart, open your mind, and honestly explore the arguments and follow the evidence wherever it clearly leads. That is what I finally did, and it made an eternal difference in my life. If you are a sincere seeker, then I encourage you to read this book, study its contents, and follow up on the suggested readings I include at the end of most of the exchanges (there is also a selected reading list at the end of the book). I pray that you will be challenged to think through your own positions and to consider thoughtfully the evidences and arguments in support of Christ's claims.

It is also my sincere prayer that the Christian believer reading this book will be strengthened in faith and will learn valuable strategies for engaging the skeptic. As you know, we are called to always be prepared to give a defense for the hope that is in our hearts, doing so with respect and a gentle spirit (1 Pet 3:15–16). For most of us, this requires much study. Christ instructs us to "love the Lord your God with all your heart and with all your soul and with all your mind" (Matt 22:37). Most Christians have heart and soul pretty well covered, but unfortunately we all do not follow up with the mind nearly as well as we should. I say this with sensitivity and respect, but I also say this as an admonishing brother in Christ. We will study the intricacies of our academic majors and our professions, but many of us will not devote the same level of mindful study to the teachings and claims of the Lord of the universe. Reflect upon that, and let your own heart and mind be convicted. Commit to the hard work of being a mindful Christian and of preparing yourself to be a defender or apologist of the hope that is in you. It is my prayer that this book will aid a new generation of deeply thinking Christians who will be ready to provide meaningful and intelligent answers to the many tough questions from the seeker, sincere questions that deserve honest answers. May we all be encouraged to engage in thoughtful yet truly open-minded explorations of the claims of Christ and the teachings of general Christian orthodoxy, what C. S. Lewis called "mere Christianity."

Exchange 1

Am I an Atheist or an Agnostic?

Hello Prof,

A friend on campus mentioned that you believe in God and that you are a Christian. I hope you don't mind that I'm e-mailing you. I've been thinking a lot about life and God lately, and I would like to ask you a few questions, again, if you don't mind. Here goes . . .

I've heard some people talk about why they believe God exists, and I've heard others explain why they don't believe God exists. I'm a little confused, because some who doubt the existence of God claim to be atheists while other doubters claim to be agnostics. What's the difference? I have to admit that I'm not so sure where I stand on all this God stuff.

Sincerely,
Seeker

Dear Seeker,

Thank you so much for your e-mail, and I'm very happy that you chose to write me. I think issues of faith are vitally important to our lives, both materially on this earth and eternally in the afterlife, because I am convinced that this earthly existence simply is not "all there is." I will do my best to answer your questions and point you toward other resources. Who knows where this will lead, but I hope we can have more exchanges, because there is much to discuss. But, I will leave that up to you. Whatever you would like to talk about is fine with me.

Your questions about *atheism* and *agnosticism* are important. By definition, *atheism* literally means "no God," "without God," or "absence of God" (*a* means without or the absence of, and *theos* means God). Therefore, in the strictest sense atheists claim there is no God. The problem, of course, is that a finite being (the atheist) cannot prove absolutely that there is no absolute being (God). Thus, atheism is untenable and self-defeating: you would basically have to be all-knowing to know that there is no all-knowing being like God. That is, you'd have to be God to know with absolute certainty that there is no God.

Because of this obvious logical problem, many atheists will claim that this is not the definition of atheism and, instead, will express a qualified position in which they say they really do not know for sure if there is a God or not (a form of agnosticism). Yet, since they think there isn't enough evidence for God, they conclude by default there is no God. This is their revised definition of atheism, but it is equally poor reasoning. It places the burden of proof only on those who need to prove the existence of God and effectively bypasses the burden of providing arguments and evidence to sustain their claim that God does not exist. See the trick? Ultimately, such atheists (though not all, to be fair) express a view without having to substantiate the view and expect their opposition to do all the intellectual heavy lifting.

The more sincere and honest route is to claim *agnosticism*, which means to not know or to be without knowledge (*a* means without and *gnosis* means knowledge). Such people claim not to know. This is a very easy position to sustain, because all you have to prove is the fact that you don't know. However, if a person is truly agnostic and doesn't know either way, the question becomes: why is he or she coming down on the side of atheism? Why not just come down on the side of theism? If you truly don't know either way, then you could just as easily be a theist as an atheist, no? Ah, but there's the rub. Most so-called agnostics really don't want there to be a God, because if they decide God exists, then they have to grapple with how this God would want his creations to live. That is, their problem with God's existence is not so much intellectual as moral: they want to live the way they want without any higher moral authority telling them what they should and should not do. Yet, they know the logical problem of claiming pure atheism (as discussed above), so they try to sidestep the complexities by claiming agnosticism. I'm not sure this really helps them.

Saint Paul, who wrote the book of Romans (this is a letter he wrote to Christians in Rome around 56 AD and is found in the New Testament of the Bible), notes that the problem isn't so much the absence of evidence but, rather, that people suppress or ignore the evidence that proves God does quite plainly exist: "For the wrath of God is revealed from heaven against all ungodliness and unrighteousness of men, who by their unrighteousness suppress the truth. For what can be known about God is plain to them, because God has shown it to them. For his invisible attributes, namely, his eternal power and divine nature, have been clearly perceived, ever since the creation of the world, in the things that have been made. So they are without excuse" (Rom 1:18–20). Therefore, the issue of the existence or nonexistence of God is more a matter of will than reason, morality than intellect.

Note, too, that many agnostics will claim not to know or will assert the inability to know anything with certainty, yet they seem to know with certainty that they cannot know. I sometimes ask such skeptics why it is that they are so sure that they do know that they cannot know anything with certainty; and, why is it that in their lack of knowledge they seem to know for sure that they cannot know at least something about God? It's rather self-defeating to claim to know with certainty that you cannot know anything for certain. Just making the claim of not knowing suggests we can know something, which then suggests we should be able to know something about the existence (or nonexistence) and nature of God.

There are plenty of reasons why some people believe in atheism, but I do not find these reasons to be compelling. I can understand having a degree of doubt rooted in a lack of knowledge. But, I do not believe there are good excuses for remaining in a state of ignorance, especially in our current age of information overload. Is it really reasonable to remain ignorant about such weighty matters and to just throw up your hands and be content with not knowing? For some people, I think it may be more an issue of fashion or preference—it's "cool" to bask in ambiguity, some tell me, and others say that there is comfort in chaos and confusion. Ambiguity and confusion may be intellectually fashionable in some circles (particularly on university campuses), but at the end of the day, these perspectives are not comfortable, nor are they reasonable.

For example, if you were to discover that your car had been stolen, would you find it comforting if the police officer you called told you that you can never really know for sure if your car was actually stolen or if you ever really had a car to begin with? In your daily life, you want assurance of knowing certain things, like who stole your car and if it can be found or not. (No doubt your insurance company will want to know with certainty.) Simply put, skeptical agnosticism is plainly unlivable. Furthermore, remaining in ignorance about the existence or nonexistence of God isn't intellectually honest or viable; there is no good excuse for not investigating the wealth of evidence that we do have. We may not be able to claim *complete* knowledge of God, but we can certainly claim *sufficient* knowledge. After my own extensive and sincere investigation of the evidence, I'm convinced that atheism is false and theism (the belief in the existence of God) is true.

Here are a few books that may help you start sorting through some of these issues more fully:

> Geisler, Norman, and Frank Turek. *I Don't Have Enough Faith to Be an Atheist*. Wheaton, IL: Crossway, 2004.
> Morris, Thomas V. *God and the Philosophers: The Reconciliation of Faith and Reason*. Oxford: Oxford University Press, 1996.
> Sproul, R. C. *The Consequences of Ideas: Understanding the Concepts that Shaped Our World*. Wheaton, IL: Crossway, 2000.
> Zacharias, Ravi. *Can Man Live without God?* Dallas: Word, 1994.
> ———. *The Real Face of Atheism*. Grand Rapids: Baker Books, 2004.

I hope this helps a bit. If you have more questions, then please do let me know. I enjoy discussing these issues, and I want to help you in your investigation of these questions.

Cheers,
Prof. Dave

Dear Prof,

Thank you so much for taking the time to address my questions. I really wasn't sure what to expect. Actually, I was expecting you not to reply at all. Now, I'm wondering what I've gotten myself into. Ha ha. Seriously, though, you've given me a few ideas to chew on here, but I'm a bit uncomfortable with your saying you know some things are *true* and other things are *false*. I've been taught that there really is no such thing as truth, and I've been told that since we really can't know anything very well we should avoid saying one person's view is true while another person's view is false. Can you please explain what you mean by *true* and *false*? Thanks.

Sincerely,
Seeker

Dear Seeker,

I can understand your hesitation, even shock, at my statements that some views are true and other views are false. It is common these days in schools and universities to teach a rather fuzzy notion of truth, and I find such instruction causes more confusion than clarity.

Let me begin answering your question by simply asking some questions back. I hope you don't mind. You say you've been taught that there is no such thing as truth. Is what you have been taught true? You say you've been taught that you ought not to say that another person's view is false. But, aren't you basically saying that you think my view is false by disagreeing with me? You mention that you are not sure that we can really know anything with much certainty. However, aren't you claiming to know something with a fair degree of certainty? (That is, you are claiming to know with certainty that you cannot know much of anything with certainty.)

Do you see where I'm heading here? For all of your good intentions of trying to avoid claiming any idea to be true or false, you are in fact making claims that you think are true, and you are implying that the views with which you disagree are false. You cannot escape truth and falsity. I think your deeper question is really this: how can we know what is true and what is false? Now, that is an important and meaningful question.

Let's explore this question by looking at the example of different religions. There are many religions, like Christianity, Judaism, Islam, and Hinduism, which teach various things about God. Though these systems agree that God exists, they do not fully agree with each other on the nature and character of that divine existence. Then, there are those religions and belief systems, like classical Buddhism, Taoism, Confucianism, and atheism, which teach there is no God per se, and these systems also disagree concerning the nature of this divine nonexistence. So, how do we know which system is right?

We begin by acknowledging that, contrary to the view expressed by popular comparative religious studies, all religions do not teach the same thing about God. For example, Christianity teaches that Christ is God, and that he died on a cross and then rose from the dead; yet, Islam teaches Christ is not God and that he never died to begin with. Pantheistic religions teach that God is immanent (that is, God is in everything around us), whereas theistic religions teach God is not immanent but, instead, transcendent (different and separate from the created world). Some religions teach there is one life, then a judgment, then an afterlife; whereas other religions teach there are multiple lives and no final judgment. Some religions teach there is good and evil, while other religions teach that good and evil are but mere illusions.

Are you beginning to see how these are contradictory teachings, and thus they all cannot be true? To claim that contradictory statements are equally true violates a fundamental law of logical thinking called the law or principle of noncontradiction. This principle basically says that two contradictory statements cannot both be true at the same time in the same way. This is a fundamental rule of good thinking, and you cannot get around it. You can deny it, but in order to deny the law of noncontradiction you have to invoke it. That is, by denying the law of noncontradiction, you are basically saying that it cannot exist *and* not exist at the same time, or that this law cannot be *both* true and false at the same time, both of which are expressions using the law of noncontradiction. Think of it this way: by denying the validity of the law of noncontradiction, you are thus saying that it is *true* that the law of noncontradiction is invalid and it is *false* that the law of noncontradiction is valid. You have used the law of noncontradiction to claim that it is not a valid logical law to use. Thus by denying it, you have affirmed it.

Therefore, the opinions or perceptions of the truth taught by the different religions are all different and often contradictory, but they cannot all be the truth. If some religious claims are true, then those claims that are the opposite must be false. Notice that we are now back to your main question—how do we know what is true and what is false? How do we know whose truth is the correct truth? Skeptics say we cannot know the truth, but this is a self-defeating position (as I mentioned above), because by claiming we cannot know the truth, the skeptic makes a knowable truth claim. It basically says we cannot know the truth, while at the same time claiming truly to know that we cannot know the truth. You see how that is self-defeating? (Please forgive the professor in me: I realize I'm repeating myself a bit. Sometimes the repetition is necessary to finally realize the main point.) It seems, therefore, that we can know some things.

The inescapable questions remain: How do we determine what is true and what is false? How do we test if a claim is true or not? This is where critical thinking comes into play. The following are some key tests for truth[1]:

1. Logical consistency: See if the claim is self-refuting or contradictory. That is, test if it violates the law of noncontradiction or commits any other error in logical thinking. If so, then there is no good logical reason to believe the statement is true. For example, if I were to say out loud, in English, "I cannot speak a word of English!" this statement would be clearly false, because I used English to say I cannot speak English. It violates the law of noncontradiction and is a false, self-defeating statement. Similarly, relativism is self-refuting and is thus false. Relativism, in its fundamental assumption, claims there is no truth. However, this statement refutes itself because it makes a truth claim even as it attempts to say there is no truth to claim. Claims that are nonsensical, that violate the law of noncontradiction, or that refute themselves fail this test for truth and are thus false.

2. Empirical adequacy: Consider if there is sufficient evidence to prove the claim. Is the evidence reliable and appropriate? Is the evidence really proving the stated conclusion? Is there counter-evidence not being presented or discussed? For example, there is no convincing or good evidence that truth is relative. Evidence can be presented demonstrating that there are many different perceptions of truth and that many different people believe many different things (often contradictory things). However, this evidence only proves that there are many different beliefs and perceptions about the truth; it does not prove that all these beliefs are equally valid and true. Basically, some perceptions of the truth can be wrong. There is a difference between truth and perceptions of truth. Truth is not determined by our perceptions of it; rather, truth is objective and independent of our subjective perceptions. If we perceive truth correctly, then our perceptions of truth

---

1. For fuller discussions of these and other tests for truth, see Geisler, *Christian Apologetics*, chapters 1–8; Geisler and Turek, *I Don't Have Enough Faith to Be an Atheist*, chapters 1–2; and Zacharias, *Can Man Live*, chapter 9 and pp. 181–84.

are correct, but if we perceive truth incorrectly, then our perceptions are false. So, this evidence (that there are many different perceptions of truth) does not prove relativism to be true. It only proves a multiplicity of perceptions.

Moreover, we can see evidence of change in moral views through time. For example, at one time abortion in America was viewed by most as an immoral act of cruel murder; now it is viewed by many as a moral choice of liberation and enlightenment. Again, this shift only proves that moral views change, but it proves nothing whatsoever about the truthfulness of the moral stance. A culture can hold a particular moral stance to be true, but the culture can be wrong in that view. As the moral view changes, the culture moves from a wrong view to a right view, or vice versa. So, again, the evidence that moral views sometimes change over time does not prove relativism to be true. It only proves that moral views change, without proving the degree of correctness of the changing views.

On the other hand, there is good evidence to prove that truth and morality are universal and absolute. For example, all cultures and religions teach basically the same thing regarding large moral issues like murder, stealing, cheating, lying, adultery, pedophilia, infanticide, and so on. Indeed, there are different cultural expressions of these moralities (how cultures deal with murderers, thieves, and liars), but all cultures teach basically the same thing about the rightness or wrongness of these actions. The empirical evidence points more conclusively to the universality and absoluteness of moral truth, and this evidence does not support the claim that morality is relative to culture or history. When considering the validity of a truth claim, carefully examine the evidence presented and make sure it is actually proving the stated conclusions

3. Experiential relevance: When analyzing a truth claim, you should also examine to what extent the claim makes sense to lived experience. Can the belief be consistently lived out? For example, moral relativism does not make sense in lived experience. When we "make it real" or try to live it out consistently, moral relativism falls apart. Let's say your friend is a moral relativist who thinks morality is culturally or individually determined, and he arrives home one afternoon to find his family has been brutally murdered, cut up into many pieces, and

spread throughout the house in a horrific display. Do you really think your friend will continue to believe truth and morality are relative? I'm fairly sure he will claim that his family has in truth been slaughtered. Do you really think he would accept the notion that it is valid for the murderer to view the family not as brutally slaughtered, but merely artistically sliced to pieces, while simultaneously it is valid for your friend to believe his family was murdered? Of course not. Moreover, your friend will most likely become a moral absolutist when he calls the police, demands justice, and insists that the murderer be found, arrested, and locked away to protect others from this evil. Would it make any practical or logical sense to say that it was both morally right and morally wrong for the murderer to have slaughtered this family? Of course not. If a claim does not make sense to lived, practical experience, then very likely the claim is false.

Why did I launch into this mini-lecture (or not-so-mini, depending on your perspective)? You are asking sincere questions, and my sense is that you are seeking real answers. Therefore, we must begin with a proper understanding of truth, and we must understand how to determine the truthfulness of various claims and perspectives. As you are analyzing different moral, religious, scientific, political, and philosophical claims, test them for truthfulness. As Socrates said, the unexamined life is not worth living. We should examine our beliefs about reality and ground our worldviews in valid presuppositions, reliable evidence, and carefully reasoned arguments.

You can use these tests for truth to determine truthfulness and falsity. Granted, it is not always easy, but it is not impossible. In my own search for truth, I have found that the fundamental precepts of Christian theism uniquely pass all of these tests, while other religious, atheistic, and agnostic views do not. In my view, there are too many logical, evidentiary, and experiential problems with atheism and agnosticism, and I cannot embrace these worldviews as true. Again, I highly recommend the following books:

> Geisler, Norman, and Frank Turek. *I Don't Have Enough Faith to Be an Atheist*. Wheaton, IL: Crossway, 2004.
> Morris, Thomas V. *God and the Philosophers: The Reconciliation of Faith and Reason*. Oxford: Oxford University Press, 1996.
> Sproul, R. C. *The Consequences of Ideas: Understanding the Concepts that Shaped Our World*. Wheaton, IL: Crossway, 2000.
> Zacharias, Ravi. *Can Man Live without God?* Dallas: Word, 1994.

———. *The Real Face of Atheism.* Grand Rapids: Baker, 2004.

Cheers,
Prof. Dave

Exchange 2

Why Do Theists Claim the Universe Had a Beginning? Isn't It Just as Reasonable to Hold to an Eternal Universe and to Believe That, Possibly, God Is the Universe?

Dear Prof,

I've heard a lot of people who believe in God, theists as you call them, say that one main reason they believe there is a God is because the universe is created, that it had a beginning. At this point, I just don't agree with the notion that we know with sufficient certainty that the material universe is created. Can't it be eternal? Isn't it true that matter can neither be created nor destroyed, thus making all matter eternal? So, if there is a God, can't we conclude that he is identical with the universe? Isn't it just as reasonable to believe that the universe is eternal or that God, if he exists, is the universe or part of the universe? Why must it be that God is distinct from the universe and that he created it? I guess what I'm looking for here is some specific evidence to sustain a belief in the existence of a Creator God. You mentioned in your previous e-mail that one test for truth is empirical adequacy. Ok, so what is some empirical evidence of God's existence?

Sincerely,
Seeker

Dear Seeker,

This is a very fair question. The overwhelming wealth of empirical, scientific evidence points to the fact that the universe is not eternal, nor is it static. There are some antitheistic thinkers (those who object to the theistic understanding of the universe) who want to believe that the universe is static and eternal so as to avoid the implications of the universe having a beginning and thus a Beginner or Creator. But, the bulk of the scientific evidence does not sufficiently support this theoretical perspective. You raise a reasonable objection to the theistic assertion that the universe is created by citing the first law of thermodynamics. Just for clarification, the common expression (which is not totally accurate as we'll see) of the first law of thermodynamics is that *energy* is neither created nor destroyed (not "matter is neither created nor destroyed"). Some pantheists and atheists misapply this first law in order to suggest the universe is eternal. They try to claim that since energy is not created nor destroyed, it must be eternally present and thus we can have an eternally present universe.

However, such a misrepresentation of this scientific law is misapplied in order to serve the antitheistic philosophical view. This law is better known as the law of conservation of energy (note, it is not called the law of the eternality of energy), and it says that the actual amount of energy in the universe is constant. What this means is that in a closed system (like the universe), energy is not added and energy is not taken away. The amount of energy is constant. This is a *descriptive* law of what is, not a *prescriptive* law of what could be or what ought to be. Basically, this law is an observation about the condition of the universe or any closed system. We do not observe energy popping into the system or leaving the system. This law says nothing about how the constant amount of energy got there to begin with. Expressing this law as "energy can neither be created nor destroyed" is a paraphrasing of the principle so as to imply that energy is eternal. Actually, this law says nothing about the eternality of energy. Notice, too, that this law does not prove that God created energy. Basically, this law cannot be used to confirm that the universe is eternal, nor can it be used to confirm that the universe had a beginning.

So, how does prevailing science prove that the universe had a beginning and thus is not itself eternal? How does science show us that since the universe had a beginning, then there must be a Creator? Buckle in, and let's take a trip around the universe.[1]

1. Information presented is a summary and collation of Geisler and Turek, *I Don't*

SECOND LAW OF THERMODYNAMICS

Again, the first law of thermodynamics cannot be used sufficiently to prove the universe is eternal, nor can it be used to prove it had a beginning. However, the second law of thermodynamics does argue in favor of the universe having a beginning. The second law is the law of entropy, which says everything tends toward disorder because the amount of usable energy is decreasing. This principle is not a contradiction of the first law but, rather, is an amplification of it. The first law says that energy is constant (i.e., that there is a fixed or limited amount), and the second law states that the amount of useable energy is decreasing and being transformed into unusable energy (note that energy is still constant; it is merely transformed from usable to unusable forms). What this means is that eventually, the universe will run down, the usable energy being transformed to unusable energy (energy is conserved, but transformed from one form to another). This is just like a moped running out of gas. The usable energy was all transformed into other forms like kinetic energy and heat. There is a conservation of energy here (first law), but the system ran down (second law). Scientists observe that the universe has a fixed amount of energy that is running down; it is moving toward a greater state of entropy. Since the universe is still running now, it could not have existed from eternity past because it would have run down already. From empirical observation and these two laws, it is scientifically reasonable to conclude that the universe had a highly ordered beginning point (commonly referred to as the singularity of the big bang) and is now running toward greater disorder (entropy). If there is a beginning point, it is reasonable to conclude, using the logical principle of causality, that there was a Beginner. (The law of causality is a principle of reasoning that states anything that had a beginning had a cause: some agent that brought the thing into existence, and that caused it to exist.) Theists view this Beginner (or Causal Agent) to be God. Applying the second law of thermodynamics and the logical law of causality, we have some evidence for the existence of God.

THE UNIVERSE IS EXPANDING

In 1916, when Einstein was developing and fine-tuning his general relativity theory, he did not like where his theory was heading. He said that he

---

Have Enough Faith to Be an Atheist, 73–84, and Geisler and Bocchino, *Unshakable Foundations*, 90–110.

found it quite unnerving that his theory, as it was originally conceived and validated by experiment and observations of the day, pointed to a beginning to time and a beginning to the universe. This logical conclusion contradicted his personal belief in an eternal universe. (He was a pantheist at that time and believed that the universe was eternal and that God was in all things.) Indeed, many scientists of that day believed the universe to be static, unchanging, and eternal—not because there was evidence to support this claim but because this model best fit their naturalistic views (the belief that all there is in the universe is matter and energy, that the nonmaterial is not real). There were plenty of scientific theories in the seventeenth, eighteenth, and nineteenth centuries that proposed a beginning to the universe, but these theories contradicted the naturalistic assumptions of many in the scientific community of the early twentieth century. Yet, Einstein's own calculations kept pointing to a beginning to the universe. Einstein himself said that he found the implications of his theory irritating. As he admitted, his irritation stemmed from his dislike for the philosophical and theological implications of his theory—that the universe is not eternal or static, that it had a beginning, and that there was some kind of eternal cause (God) to the universe.

In 1919, British cosmologist Arthur Eddington conducted experiments during a solar eclipse that confirmed Einstein's general relativity theory and further substantiated the conclusion that the universe was not static but had a beginning. Yet, Eddington, like Einstein, was unhappy with his findings and stated that the philosophical implications of his findings were repugnant to him and that he wanted to find a genuine loophole to get around this conclusion. Now, this doesn't sound like objective science to me. Rather, this is evidence of how certain presuppositions are determining how facts are being interpreted, and how a logical truth is being rejected not based on intellectual reasons but because of the reasoners' will or personal desire—they do not *want* the implications of their findings to be true.

By 1922 Russian mathematician Alexander Friedmann exposed Einstein's cosmological constant (now known as the "fudge factor") as an algebraic error—in his desire to avoid acknowledging that the universe had a beginning, Einstein actually divided by zero! At this time, Dutch astronomer Willem de Sitter also concluded that the general relativity theory required the universe to have a beginning and that the universe had to be expanding from a singular point in time. And in 1927, astronomer

Edwin Hubble actually observed red shifts in the universe that indicated galaxies are moving away from the observer and thus the universe is expanding from a beginning point in space and time, just as Einstein's theory predicted. Then in 1929, Einstein went to Hubble's observatory, saw the evidence for himself, and realized it was undeniable. He admitted that the cosmological constant was the greatest blunder of his scientific career. Ultimately, scientific theory (general relativity) predicted a beginning to time and an expanding universe, and observation confirmed these predictions, strongly suggesting that the universe had a beginning and was created. If it had a beginning and was created, then it is reasonable to conclude there is a Creator.

RADIATION FROM THE BIG BANG

In 1948, scientists theorized that if the big bang really happened, then there should be some kind of detectable radiation from that significant cosmic blast. It wasn't until 1965 that scientists Arno Penzias and Robert Wilson accidentally discovered this predicted radiation. At first, they thought there were bird droppings in their New Jersey Bell Labs antenna array causing interference in their readings, so they had it cleaned off. But the radiation was still being detected, no matter where they tuned their antenna. This discovery won them the Nobel prize, because it was one of the greatest of discoveries—the actual radiation afterglow from the big bang. This discovery adds more empirical evidence that the universe had a beginning and makes it much more difficult to have faith in the steady state theory of an eternal universe (the belief that the universe "just is" and has always just existed). I find the evidence thus far for the beginning of the universe and thus a Beginner (i.e., God) to be quite convincing. But there's more.

GALAXY SEEDS

Given the existence of this background radiation, scientists postulated that there should be slight variations in temperature in this radiation or ripples, and these ripples would allow for matter to congregate by gravitational forces into galaxies. In 1989, NASA launched the COBE space probe in search of these ripples, which were then discovered in 1992. Not only were the ripples detected, but scientists discovered the immense congregation of matter that formed into galaxies. Also, they discovered that the initial big bang explosion and resulting expansion were precisely tuned, such that it allowed for just the right amount of matter to congregate to form galaxies without the universe collapsing back on itself. George Smoot, the director of the COBE program, remarked that this discovery was like looking at the very face of God. Michael Turner, astrophysicist of the University of Chicago, said this was the Holy Grail of cosmology. And Stephen Hawking said this was the most significant discovery, possibly ever. Again, this mounting empirical evidence further substantiates the theist's claim that the universe indeed had a beginning and thus a Beginner.

EINSTEIN'S GENERAL THEORY OF RELATIVITY

Finally, Einstein's general theory of relativity, which has been repeatedly confirmed, demands a beginning to time, space, and matter. This theory is supported by the evidence for the big bang, and it predicted the expanding universe, the radiation afterglow, and the galaxy seeds, which all have been discovered. Combined with the second law of thermodynamics, there is powerful, overwhelming evidence that the universe is not eternal but in fact had a beginning. And if it had a beginning, then using the logical principle of causality we can conclude that it must have a Beginner or a Creator.

Most scientists, including Hawking, all agree that it is logical and reasonable to conclude that if the universe had a beginning then there must be a Creator. This is the basic law of causality, and science is built upon this law (i.e., the purpose of science is to find causes of events). To deny the causality of the universe is to fly in the face of science itself and merely points to the fact that some people simply don't *want* the universe to have a beginning, because they don't *like* the ramifications of there being a God. Their disbelief, then, is not one of reason, logic, and science; rather, it is one of sheer will and a faith in impossible or insufficiently supported theories.

In the light of this compelling evidence, there are still some scientists who are seeking other possible explanations, again not because the evidence for other explanations is there, but because they do not want there to be a beginning to the universe and thus a God of the universe. For example, there are the cosmic rebound theory, the theory of endless parallel universes, the imaginary time theory (thus no need to say time had a beginning, yet note the operative word in the name of this theory is *imaginary*), string theory, and a few other wonderfully imaginative theories. But, these theories are not based upon observable fact or hard empirical evidence; they are creative theoretical fictions, and at some point they violate one or both of the first two laws of thermodynamics, or they violate other basic scientific principles (like causality). (For detailed analyses of these alternate theories, see the suggested resources below.)

So, we can either put our faith in the creation of the universe out of nothing by God, which is so strongly confirmed by the second law of thermodynamics, the fact of the expanding universe, the presence of the background radiation glow from the big bang, the existence of radiation ripples and galaxy seeds, and the general theory of relativity; or, we can choose to put our faith in imaginative theories that are not sufficiently supported by observable evidence and that are created out of a desire not to know the truth but to avoid the truth that science shows us. For me, it just takes too much faith to believe that the universe is static or eternal and to deny that the universe had a beginning. I just don't have that much faith. But don't take my word for it. Check out some of these other resources:

> Craig, William Lane. "The Ultimate Question of Origins: God and the Beginning of the Universe." *Leadership U.* http://www.leaderu.com/offices/billcraig/docs/ ultimatequestion.html.
> Craig, William Lane, and Quentin Smith. *Theism, Atheism and Big Bang Cosmology.* Oxford: Oxford University Press, 1993.
> *Does God Exist?: William Lane Craig and Anthony Flew Debate.* DVD. (Norcross, GA: Ravi Zacharias International Ministries, 1998).
> Geisler, Norman L., and Peter Bocchino. *Unshakable Foundations: Contemporary Answers to Crucial Questions about the Christian Faith.* Minneapolis: Bethany, 2001.
> Geisler, Norman L., and Frank Turek. *I Don't Have Enough Faith to Be an Atheist.* Wheaton, IL: Crossway, 2004.
> Jastrow, Robert. *God and the Astronomers.* 2nd ed. New York: Norton, 1992.
> Moreland, J. P., and Kai Nielsen. *Does God Exist?* Amherst, NY: Prometheus, 1993.
> Strobel, Lee. *The Case for a Creator.* Grand Rapids: Zondervan, 2004.
> *What Is the Evidence for/against the Existence of God?* Debate between William Lane Craig and Peter W. Atkins. DVD. (Norcross, GA: Ravi Zacharias International Ministries, 1998).

This may seem like a lot of information all at once. But in the very least, I think we can agree that it is becoming more difficult for us to say that there simply isn't enough evidence out there for us to consider carefully.

I hope this encourages you to dig deeper and to investigate some of this material yourself.

Cheers,
Prof. Dave

Exchange 3

Can't Some Things Be Created by Chance?

Dear Prof,

I was reading an essay about the beginning of the universe and theistic views of science. I'm finding compelling reasons to think that theism and science do not necessarily contradict each other. However, I think that to argue for either extreme (all God or all chance) is silly. We can see random chance operating every day, and at the same time we can stand in awe of the fact that God created the universe. When I say we can see chance things happening every day, I mean that randomness and probability seem to have some effect on things. Chromosomes mistakenly pair up and create malformed babies. Are mistakes and random chance one of God's methods of creating life, namely cell formation? Does he control every cell division? Every DNA strand replication? Every mutation? Does he control all such minute events, or did he establish the mechanisms for creation and then stand back to watch it run on its own? I wonder whether God micromanages all of existence and has his hand in every single thing—even the toss of a dice—or whether he built the apparatus and watches it go or, sometimes, guides things along their way.

Sincerely,
Seeker

Dear Seeker,

The issue of creation by chance alone or God alone is largely in reference to the origins of the universe and the origins of life. So, in that sense, we only have the two extremes: (1) the universe came into being by chance; or (2) the universe was created by a necessary being, what theists call God. (Note, in our previous exchange we refuted the third possible option of the universe being eternally existent.) To me, the first option is somewhat nonsensical, because *chance* is an expression of mathematical probability, not a causal agent. Also, it is equally nonsensical to conclude that nature (the natural universe) can come from nothing on its own via natural causes alone without being caused by a force outside of nature (this requires nature to preexist itself to bring itself into being, which is nonsensical). By extension, it seems to me equally unreasonable to believe that mind (which you and I experience and are using in these very exchanges) can come into being on its own from mindlessness—mere matter—through mindless natural causes.

However, the second option (the universe, life, and mind came into being via the work of an external necessary being, or God) satisfies the logical first principle of causality, fits with the empirical evidence from science we discussed in the previous exchange, and coalesces with what we've come to expect in the real world through our common lived experience. I think it is unreasonable to hold that the existence of the universe, life, and the mind happened by chance; but it is quite logical and reasonable to maintain that God (a personal agent that is above and outside the created universe and who possesses mind) created everything. Moreover, it is reasonable to conclude that God is actually intimately involved with everything he has created, because he is a personal being (because humans are personal and relational, and it only makes sense that we would be created by a personal, relational being).

Let's talk a bit more about this issue of chance as a creative force. I would argue that we never see chance creating or doing anything, at least not in the way most people use this word *chance*. Again, *chance* is a term of mathematical probability; it is not a causal agent that causes things to occur. Indeed, we do see low-probability events occurring by what appears to be pure chance, as with mutations in cell division or with that one sperm out of millions that fertilizes an ovum. But, there is a mechanism already in place, which had to be designed beforehand, that allows for this possibility to occur, regardless of how improbable. The so-called chance occurrence did not happen randomly, out of the blue, arbitrarily, for no reason whatsoever (which many people imply by their use of the term *chance*). In the case of mutation and malformation in gene sequencing, for example, these biological events do not happen by chance in the sense that, oops, it just arbitrarily happened for no reason whatsoever. Rather, there is a molecular and genetic possibility for mutation to occur, because of the preexistence of a designed genetic mechanism that allows for a range of sequencing to occur.

Given certain circumstances, there are occurrences that are far more probable than others, but the highly improbable are still possible. (Note that from a biblical theistic perspective, malformation became a part of design under the curse of sin. There are theists who do not hold to this view, but biblical theism argues that the original biological design was corrupted by the consequences of sin.) In this sense, mutation does not really happen by chance. Rather, what has happened is that the highly improbable has occurred, but this occurrence is all part of the realm of possibility as determined by the designed system and its current condition. These chance events do not lead to anything unexpected within the context of the designed system. Moreover, such events cannot lead to something greater than or other than the intentional design of the system itself. That is, these chance events cannot lead to new systems or new life. You see, for an event to even occur, it must first be possible for it to occur, and for things to be possible, there must be a designed mechanism to allow for the possible to occur. And, these designed systems do not morph, by accident, into some fundamentally different system.

Now, what about your question regarding God's involvement with the world on a micro level? I would argue that it is not inconceivable for God providentially to micromanage everything. In our past exchanges we discussed the wealth of evidence for the existence of God, and it may help at this point to provide a little more information about the Christian theistic understanding of the nature of God. By no means is the following an exhaustive description, but it is a meaningful one that is relevant to our discussion here.

God is the uncaused causal agent. That is, he is not an effect; rather, he is the eternal agent that was not caused, because he is not an effect. According to the first principle of causality, only effects have causes. Think of it this way: there could never be a time or a moment in all of reality when there was truly nothing in existence. Nothing comes from nothing, so if there were ever a time when there was truly nothing, then nothing could ever be. Therefore, there must be a necessary being that has always existed who is the causal agent for the created universe as we know it. God is that necessary being who caused or brought the universe (an effect) and everything in the universe (also effects) into being. Moreover, we can reasonably know that God is more than a nameless, faceless, blind, impersonal causal agent, because all things that he created must in some way express or be representative of aspects of his own nature. That is, the things God creates cannot be greater than himself. So, such things as mind, personality, emotions, free will, morality, and so on are aspects of his creation, because they are also aspects of his being or nature. (Think about it—a nonthinking, impersonal, emotionless, nonfree, amoral being could not create beings with minds, personality, emotions, free will, and morality.) Thus, it is reasonable to say that God is personal and can be known or related to on a personal level.

Moreover, when we consider the anthropic constants in the universe (those finely tuned constants that must exist in perfect balance in order for human life to exist on earth), it makes sense to surmise that this Creator God (the Necessary Causal Being) is a caring, loving God who has designed such a complex and intricate universe to support life on earth generally but also to support highly complex life with a desire to know the Creator, with minds to seek out this Creator, and with the opportunity to discover evidence for the Creator. It is interesting to note that the earth seems uniquely positioned to allow for humans to observe evidences in the universe that point to this Creator God.[1] From this logical reasoning, Christian theists conclude that God is the necessary causal being who has always existed. He was not himself created or caused and is thus by nature infinite in wisdom, power, intelligence, knowledge, and love.

Given God's infinite nature, it is indeed possible that God is micromanaging everything. The Bible speaks of God's intimate knowledge, care, and concern for everything. For example, we are told that God knows and cares for each individual sparrow, has counted the hairs on our heads, holds us more valuable than sparrows, and thus is intimately concerned with the minutiae of our daily lives (Matt 10:29–31). We are told that God knit us in the womb, that we are wonderfully and fearfully made, and that he knows our metaphysical being before we are given material substance (Ps 139). This clearly indicates that God is involved with all aspects of our person and our coming into being. Also, the discovery of more anthropic

1. See Gonzales and Richards, *Privileged Planet*.

constants in the universe attests not only to the fine-tuned nature of the universe but also to the intimacy of the Designer, that he is most likely maintaining this universe constantly. Moreover, the Apostle Paul reminds us that God gives us life, breath, and all things and that in him we live, move, and exist (Acts 17:25–28), which suggests that God is maintaining us physically and spiritually.

So, I don't think it is totally unrealistic to believe that God is in fact providentially sustaining and maintaining all things on multiple levels, including the molecular. Our finite minds have difficulty comprehending this possibility, but as we know, truth and reality are not dependent upon our finite minds. Our understanding is limited by our finite minds, but objective truth and reality themselves are not limited by nor contingent upon our minds. We have to be careful to avoid the blind watchmaker analogy for God. This is a deistic view, that God has wound up the universe, has established the various natural laws and physical rules, and has let it go unguided and unattended until it naturally winds down. This concept falsely presumes an impersonal God and negates the necessity of Christ coming to redeem that which we have destroyed (the created order, ourselves, and our relationship with God) through our own sin or rebellion against God.

I hope this helps somewhat. You may be interested in the following resources that explain these and other related topics in more detail:

> Behe, Michael, ed. *Science and Evidence for Design in the Universe.* Ft. Collins, CO: Ignatius, 2000.
>
> Broom, Neil. *How Blind Is the Watchmaker?: Nature's Design and the Limits of Naturalistic Science.* 2nd ed. Downers Grove, IL: InterVarsity, 2001.
>
> Gonzales, Guillermo, and Jay Richards. *The Privileged Planet: How Our Place in the Cosmos Is Designed for Discovery.* Washington, DC: Regnery, 2004.
>
> Meyer, Stephen C. *Signature in the Cell: DNA and the Evidence for Intelligent Design.* New York: HarperOne, 2009.
>
> Moreland, J. P., and Kai Nelson. *Does God Exist?: The Debate Between Theists and Atheists.* Amherst: Prometheus Books, 1993.
>
> Strobel, Lee. *The Case for a Creator.* Grand Rapids: Zondervan, 2004.

Cheers,
Prof Dave

Exchange 4

Isn't Evolution an Adequate Scientific Explanation for the Origins of Life?

Dear Prof,

Thanks for that last response. You've given me some things to think about. What you say does make some sense, but I'm not so sure I'm ready to accept that the universe was created by a personal God or a supreme power. After all, doesn't the theory of evolution provide a sound scientific explanation for the origins of life? If evolution is true, then do we really need God or some supreme power to be what you called the necessary being or the first cause of the universe and life?

Thank you for your patience, by the way, and for taking my questions seriously. I really do appreciate it.

Sincerely,
Seeker

Dear Seeker,

You are very welcome! It is my pleasure having these exchanges with you. Your questions are very important, and much is riding on the answers. This exchange reminds me of a passage in one of my favorite science fiction novels, *A Canticle for Leibowitz* by Walter M. Miller Jr. In the second section of that book, titled "Fiat Lux" ("Let there be light"), a university scholar is arguing with Dom Paulo, the abbot of a monastery, about the proper study of history and knowledge. Dom Paulo at one point says, "Men must fumble awhile with error to separate it from truth, I think—as long as they don't seize the error hungrily because it has a pleasanter taste."[1] So true, don't you think? We must ask good questions and seek the answers that are true, regardless of whether we find them pleasant or not. This is what I have attempted to do in my own exploration of Christian theism.

I used to believe in evolution to some degree, and I tried to reconcile my belief in evolution and my belief in God as Creator. (Note that the word *belief* is appropriately used in both cases, for the Darwinian evolutionist must have faith as does the believer in God. As I hope our discussions will show, I think it takes much more faith to be an evolutionist than a Christian theist.) The more I studied the science of evolution, the more I began to see that macroevolution (as commonly taught and generically called evolution) is contradictory, violates some basic principles of science, violates logic, and ultimately is not consistently supported by the evidence. Interestingly, Darwin himself pointed out the main problem with his theory—that it is not supported by the fossil record. He hoped that in generations to come, more fossil discoveries would prove his theory.[2] Quite the contrary: paleontology continues to raise serious doubts about evolution, leading many thinkers to conclude the theory is seriously wanting if not entirely wrong. Major evolutionists, like the late Stephen Jay Gould, confirmed that paleontology does not provide empirical evidence in support of evolution. Note that this reality motivated Gould to develop the theory of punctuated equilibrium to make the fossil record fit his own evolutionary perspective[3] and to try to divert attention away from the real ramifications of the fossil record—that some Intelligence must have created separate kinds of animals. Also, Darwin noted that if science can demonstrate that there are irreducibly complex systems or organisms that cannot develop gradually, then his theory would be in big trouble.[4] Cell biology and discoveries in DNA show us that there are many irreducibly complex systems whose individual components cannot exist in isolation and require the whole system to exist simultaneously for them to function. Evolution cannot explain the existence of these irreducibly complex mechanisms, and many scientists (known as intelligent design scientists) argue that the presence of these irreducibly complex systems scientifically

1. Miller, *Canticle*, 236–37.
2. Darwin, *Origins*, 317.
3. See, for example, Gould's "Is a New and General Theory of Evolution Emerging?" in *Dinosaur in a Haystack*; and see also his *Structure of Evolutionary Theory*.
4. Fowler and Kuebler, *Evolution Controversy*, 56–57.

disproves evolution, as per Darwin's criteria. So, just from a scientific perspective alone, there is good reason not to believe macroevolution. (Note that microevolution is observable and true, but it is not the same as macroevolution, nor is microevolution the mechanism by which macroevolution supposedly operates.)

The evolution controversy boils down to an interesting matter of faith, for proponents of both sides. It's interesting to note that humans, with all of our sophistication, intelligence, imagination, and design capabilities, are not intelligent enough or capable enough to design or create life or complex systems comparable to the life and biological systems we see around us, from the most basic single-celled life to the most advanced human being. Yet, evolutionists would have us believe that nature is an active, creative agent. Even though nature has no intelligence, mind, or will, and thus cannot plan or design in anticipation of certain conditions in which organisms should exist, evolutionists want us to believe that nonliving, unthinking, blind forces of nature gave rise to life forms that have the ability to live, think, feel, plan, and exercise free will through a mind. It takes way too much faith in the absence of clear and convincing evidence to believe this theory (that nonlife can give rise to life, that nonemotion can give rise to emotion, and that nonmind can give rise to mind). I have to ask, now, who is relying on blind faith and who is seeking to understand the world in terms of science, logic, and reason? It does not seem so unreasonable to conclude that life, emotion, mind, and will are all the creation of a supremely intelligent, emotional, and personal divine agent—God.

To be sure, the conclusion that macroevolution is a flawed theory and does not adequately explain the existence and diversity of life was very tough for me to accept. I was steeped in evolutionary thought—it's hard not to be, growing up in a secular world, being uncritically taught this theory, and having it assumed to be true. It's interesting how Darwinian evolution has become dogma for the secularists, atheists, and naturalists these days. For all the rhetoric they advance against religiosity, faith, and belief, they show the most rigid religiosity I've ever witnessed. Darwin is viewed as a god of science, and his theories are like holy writ. Remember that evolution is only a theory, and all theories are by definition open to review and scientific debate; yet evolution is one scientific theory that the secularists don't allow to be debated. The groups I've mentioned believe Darwin's theories dogmatically, and they charge any nonbelievers with heresy, exercising an evolutionist type of inquisition, renouncing all opposition and labeling disagreement as unthinking, moronic heresy. I've even heard it asserted by teachers and professors that Darwinian evolution has been so well established in the scientific community that it is no longer theory but fact. The assumption, then, is that there need be no more discussion or debate over evolution. Those scientists who try to examine and critique it are ridiculed, dismissed, and often denied publication or even tenure. (Now who is being unfair and closed-minded?)

Coming from the evolutionist view myself, when I started to learn about the problems of evolution, I experienced the disquieting results of a paradigm shift. It was like the world was being turned upside down. But, when I carefully considered the evidence, I became comforted in the truth, and my mind and understanding were freed from the bondage of narrow thinking and blind faith in a false theory. The truth does, indeed, set one free.

Remember, ideas have consequences, and there have been many horrific consequences engendered by evolutionary thinking. Darwinian evolution denies (or in the very least does not require) the existence of God and thus removes him from the center of all meaning, purpose, and value. Also, evolutionary thinking at best only describes the advanced nature of humanity without ascribing any special value to the human. The result is moral relativism, dehumanization, racism, oppression of the poor (social Darwinism of the nineteenth century that said the poor will be selected out because they are not fit to survive socially and economically), and eugenics (selective breeding of humans and the killing of "unfit" humans to improve the species, one perpetrator of eugenics being Adolf Hitler). Not everyone who believes in evolution supports these horrific ideologies, but the point is that these ideas are the logical outworking of evolutionary thought. It is important that we think through what we believe, why we believe it, and what the consequences of that belief are. There is still much to be examined and critiqued in the Darwinian theory of evolution. By no means is it settled science, and by no means is macroevolution scientific fact.

Cheers,
Prof. Dave

Hey Prof,

Whoa, wait a minute. Are you really trying to say that evolution is not settled science? That sounds a bit too radical for me. Doesn't this theory basically acknowledge that all life is made up of the same four basic components in DNA, only arranged in different orders? Therefore, isn't it feasible that mutations can alter the combinations of DNA structures and cause new life forms to be created and thus produce speciation? Also, don't most evolutionists now argue that evolution is not necessarily "progressive," but that it basically gives rise to different life forms, some that survive and some that do not? As such, can't we conclude that evolution is not perfect and does not necessarily give rise to "better" organisms but that it just gives rise to new and different organisms, some that survive and some that do not?

Sincerely,
Seeker

Dear Seeker,

In reality, DNA is much more complex than what you describe. In fact, open-minded scientific inquiry shows us that DNA is an irreducibly complex system. As we know, thanks to Watson and Crick at our own Cold Spring Harbor Labs just down the street from us here in Old Westbury, DNA is a complex molecule with a double helix structure that is like a twisting ladder. The sides are formed by alternating deoxyribose and phosphate molecules, and the rungs are composed of specific orders of four different nitrogen bases—A (adenine), T (thymine), C (cytosine), and G (guanine). These nitrogen bases are essentially four different letters in the genetic alphabet, and these letters are combined in specific and complex ways in order to communicate a very specific message that allows for life to exist and function.

If you sat down at the table and found a bowl of alphabet soup with letters randomly mixed in the bowl, you'd think nothing of it. But, if you found spelled out in the bowl, "John, after you finish eating this soup, please wash the bowl," you would have no problem concluding that this string of letters was not a random act, that it was a message, that there was meaning to this message, that there was intentionality behind it (an agent intended to communicate a specific message in a specific way to a recipient who was equipped to decipher the message), that there was intelligent design behind it, and that there was therefore an intelligent designer behind the message (like, maybe, your mom). Let's look at just the nucleus of an amoeba (a very "simple," single-celled organism). If you take the four genetic letters (A, T, C, and G) and spell them all out in normal printing font, the information in the nucleus of the amoeba would fill 30 volumes of the *Encyclopedia Britannica*. If you spelled out all the letters of all the DNA of the *entire* simple amoeba, the letters would fill 1,000 complete volumes of the *Encyclopedia Britannica*. More importantly, DNA isn't just random arrangements of letters. Rather, these letters are arranged in a very specific order, and they communicate vast amounts of specific and meaningful information, just like a real volume of an encyclopedia.

Arguing just from this example of a single-celled organism, it is nonsensical to suggest that a blind, unthinking, and unreasoning natural process like natural selection or mutation can give rise to such specified complexity. It is interesting and telling that people looking for intelligent life in the universe believe that a simple string of prime numbers coming from a radio signal from deep in space would constitute evidence of intelligence having sent that signal. Yet, the same people who hold to an evolutionary worldview simultaneously conclude that the complex string of information in the DNA of an amoeba (comparable to 1,000 volumes of an encyclopedia) somehow does not reveal evidence of intelligent design! You'd have to have a lot of faith to believe that.

In my view, it is not feasible that unguided, unthinking, blind mutation of DNA leads to speciation. (And, by the way, this is granting the existence of the DNA to begin with—mutation and natural selection cannot explain the origin of DNA.) First, this creative process via mutation is not observable in nature. For example, whenever the AIDS virus mutates, the result is always a mutated AIDS virus. When bacteria mutates, the product is always a bacteria, only changed. Scientists use fruit flies in genetic experiments because their short life spans allow for ease of studying genetic variation over hundreds of generations. All intentional mutations of fruit flies, guided by the intelligent researchers, always result in modified fruit flies, nothing else. Mutation does not add new genetic information, which is required for a new species to develop. Moreover, there is the problem of genetic limits that do not allow for speciation to occur. There are built-in genetic limits or barriers between species or organism types. Dog breeding is a good example. For all the best intentions, plans, and designs of dog breeders, their intelligently directed interventions in breeding have never led to a new species. If dog breeders and fruit fly scientists with all of their intentionality and intelligence cannot break the genetic barrier between species, then it is not feasible to think that blind natural forces, such as mutation, which exhibit no intelligence and no intentional planning, can do so.

Finally, you are right that evolution, when defined simply and generically as change, does not necessarily mean *progressive* change and that mutation can involve devolution. And, in observable nature, devolution is the only kind of change that we witness. All mutation leads to devolution, by making the organism more specialized and/or by destroying or removing information from the system. Never do we see mutation adding information to the system, which is required to break the genetic barrier between species and organism kinds.

However, macroevolution by definition is a progressive theory. That is, macroevolution says that organisms develop from less complex to more complex organisms by blind, natural processes. This is what the theory claims. Notice that this very definition violates the second law of thermodynamics, which says that systems naturally move from a state of order to disorder. In other words, if left on its own, nature cannot go from less complex to more complex without some external force acting in meaningful, intelligent ways upon the system to bring about a progressive movement. Moreover, natural selection is blind and devoid of intelligence, so it cannot make meaningful choices, nor can it guide or direct change. In order to make a progressive change, there must be an intelligence that discerns what needs to be changed in order to accomplish the progressive goal. And, there must be a goal in mind to be achieved, a way to determine how to achieve the goal, and a way to determine if the goal has been achieved or not. All of this goal-setting and goal assessment requires intelligent agency. Evolutionary discourse wrongly ascribes all kinds of volitional agency to nature. Just listen to a Discovery Channel program on prehistoric life, and you'll hear volitional agency ascribed to nature and evolution. For example, the sentence, "Nature selected this species for survival," which is a common linguistic construction of evolutionists, is totally ridiculous: nature cannot select anything, because it has no mind, intelligence, or will to make choices. Cyclical change within species supports microevolution but can never prove macroevolution.

Note that assigning volition to blind forces is just the beginning of the logical and scientific problems present in macroevolution theory. The lack of fossil evidence for transitional forms casts macroevolution in serious doubt. What we see in the fossil record is that a species suddenly appears, mutations and change occur within the species without producing another species, and then the species becomes suddenly extinct. The inability to determine ancestral relationship from fossils undermines the feasibility of macroevolution. Ninety-nine percent of the biological makeup of an organism, which is what would reveal ancestral relationship, is found in soft tissue, which is not available in fossils; macroevolutionists work with only one percent of the required material and thus make up the rest as they see fit, a highly problematic methodology at best.

The nonviability of transitional forms also makes macroevolution unfeasible and highly unlikely. Organisms are composed of multiple systems that are irreducibly complex: without all the systems in place, the organism can't exist. Transitional forms of one organism that represent its conversion to another organism could not survive, because each of these systems would need to coexist or evolve simultaneously and instantaneously for the new organism to operate. The whole idea of transitional forms is therefore a major problem for macroevolutionary theory, and indeed, although we have countless fossil remains of thousands of various species of animals, we have not one uncontested, convincing, complete fossil of a transitional creature.

Molecular isolation is yet another huge problem for macroevolution. If we share a common ancestry, say fish=>amphibian=>reptile=>mammal, then there should be evidence on the molecular level of some transitional components, shared protein sequences, and the like; however, on the molecular level there is no evidence of clear, uncontested relationship—all these animal types are molecularly isolated from each other.

To recap, macroevolution has many serious problems, and it is no wonder that many ardent evolutionary acolytes want to silence the intelligent design scientists who have been revealing these remarkable problems and causing so much anxiety within the scientific community. If you do away with macroevolution, intelligent design becomes the best game in town. In my view, intelligent design is more completely supported by the wealth of scientific evidence currently available than macroevolution. But, if we accept intelligent design, then we have to accept an Intelligent Designer (just like cosmologists are forced to accept a Creator if they accept the big bang theory as true), and this is exactly what most evolutionists do not want to do. So, once again, it all boils down to an issue of willfully not accepting the truth of the evidence. The most ardent evolutionists don't want there to be a God, so they reject intelligent design and all other challenges to their evolutionary thought.

I realize I've made many claims and arguments here, but please don't just take my word for it. Check out the following resources for more detailed information and discussions of these issues:

Behe, Michael, J. *Darwin's Black Box: The Biochemical Challenge to Evolution.* New York: Free Press, 1998.

Dembski, William A. *The Design Revolution: Answering the Toughest Questions about Intelligent Design.* Downers Grove, IL: InterVarsity, 2004.

———. *Intelligent Design: The Bridge between Science and Theology.* Downers Grove, IL: InterVarsity, 2002.

———, ed. *Uncommon Dissent: Intellectuals Who Find Darwinism Unconvincing.* Wilmington: ISI, 2004.

Dembski, William A., and James Kushiner, eds. *Signs of Intelligence: Understanding Intelligent Design.* Grand Rapids: Brazos, 2001.

Fowler, Thomas B., and Daniel Kueber. *The Evolution Controversy: A Survey of Competing Theories.* Grand Rapids: Baker, 2007.

Hunter, Cornelius G. *Darwin's God: Evolution and the Problem of Evil.* Grand Rapids: Brazos, 2002.

———. *Darwin's Proof: The Triumph of Religion over Science.* Grand Rapids: Brazos, 2003.

———. *Science's Blind Spot: The Unseen Religion of Scientific Naturalism.* Grand Rapids: Brazos, 2007.

Johnson, Phillip. *Darwin on Trial.* 2nd ed. Downers Grove, IL: InterVarsity, 1993.

Simmons, Geoffrey. *What Darwin Didn't Know: A Doctor Dissects the Theory of Evolution.* Eugene, OR: Harvest House, 2004.

Wells, Jonathan. *Icons of Evolution: Science or Myth? Why Much of What We Teach about Evolution Is Wrong.* Washington, DC: Regnery, 2002.

Cheers,
Prof. Dave

Exchange 5

But Isn't Theistic Creation Just a Mindless God-of-the-Gaps Idea?

Dear Prof,

Our previous e-mail exchange was pretty heavy and detailed, and I have to admit that I haven't fully digested all of it. I also haven't been able to get to the resources you listed, but they are definitely on my "to read" list. As I'm thinking about these various issues of creation, origins of life, and evolution, I can't help but recall what some of my biology professors have said about creation theories and Intelligent Design—that these are not really sciences and these theories resort to mindless God-of-the gaps explanations. I want to be fair to your position, but I think my bio profs have a point here. What do you think?

Sincerely,
Seeker

Dear Seeker,

Thank you for raising this issue, as it is an important question. "God-of-the-gaps" is usually an objection made by evolutionists and secularists against theists, saying that whenever there is a gap in knowledge or something that hasn't yet been explained, theists just throw in God as the ultimate answer. Indeed, some unthinking theists do this, but so too do evolutionists. Whenever evolutionists have no answer for something, they often invoke natural selection or mutation. I call this "Darwin-of-the-gaps."

My understanding of intelligent design and well-developed creation science is that these theories are not simply God-of-the-gaps theories. That is, these theorists and scientists are not simply invoking God when they do not understand something. Rather, they start with the premise that there is a God who creates, and they follow a scientific method that is open to both natural causes and supernatural causes in order to come to a more complete understanding of how God created the universe, life, and the various natural laws operating in observable reality. Methodological naturalism, which is essentially antitheistic, excludes the supernatural as a philosophical presupposition and thus prejudicially assumes that there can only be natural causes for natural events. In my opinion, this is a limited view that can only bring us partial knowledge.

Methodological naturalism asserts as an operational assumption that there is no supernatural causation in the universe and thus restricts its inquiry and conclusions to natural causation only. This scientific perspective skips proving the nonexistence of the supernatural, and merely assumes it from the beginning. On the other hand, theistic science opens itself to the possibility of both natural and supernatural causation. Just like methodological naturalism (or antitheistic science), theistic science uses inductive reasoning and the scientific method of collecting data, testing hypotheses, and making informed and reasonable inferences from the available data. Theistic science deals with the same evidence, the same facts, and the same universe that is empirically observable. But, facts do not interpret themselves. Methodological naturalism uses one set of assumptions and principles when interpreting facts (assumptions that do not allow for the supernatural), while theistic sciences use a more open or broad set of assumptions and principles that allow for both natural causation and supernatural causation. I find theistic science to be more open-minded and inclusive.

It is also important to note that theists in general and the Christian community specifically are not fully unified on the validity of the theory of evolution. There are Christians and theists who believe in a form of evolution called theistic evolution, which generally holds that God created life using evolutionary processes over long periods of time. There are other biblical theists who reject evolution altogether and believe that God created a few complex kinds of organisms that gradually developed into the variety of species through observable natural selection or microchanges, also called microevolution. As with any theory, these theistic theories are varied and nuanced. However, when we study these theistic perspectives, I think we can agree that they are not merely God-of-the-gaps theories. What follows are some thoughts and observations that you may want to think about as you sort through theistic views of the origin and diversification of life as compared to evolutionary and Darwinian views.

1. Macroevolution versus microevolution: It is important to distinguish between macroevolution and microevolution. Natural selection and mutation are indeed real and observable natural phenomena and fall under the category of microevolution. We do observe microchanges in organisms, but we do not observe organisms changing from one type of species into another. We do not have unambiguous, clear, and specific evidence in observable nature for macroevolution. The theory of macroevolution is an extrapolation from microevolution, an equivocal argument made by analogy to microevolution. The assertion is made, without clear and unambiguous evidence, that since we see microevolutionary changes within organisms, it is therefore possible that over time in the unobservable past there have been macroevolutionary changes that brought about the diversity of living organisms.

2. Genetic barriers: Not only is there a lack of clear and unambiguous evidence in observable nature for macroevolution, but there is plenty of evidence strongly suggesting that macroevolution cannot occur. Michael Behe's research into biochemistry focuses, among other things, on the genetic barriers between species. For example, scientists (who obviously have the mental capacity of intentional planning and thought) have altered the DNA of fruit flies in thousands of ways, but they have not been able to produce anything other than a modified fruit fly. It does not make rational sense to suggest that unthinking nature can change DNA and produce a new species, when thinking scientists try with the purpose of creating something new and cannot. Scientists run up against the genetic barrier between species, and so too does nature.

Another point to consider is that all mutations naturally result in loss of information or loss of functionality. Indeed, a strain of bacteria can become resistant to an antibiotic through mutation, but this new strain of bacteria is not a "super bacteria"; rather, it is more specialized and can survive in the new environment that contains the antibiotic. But, when placed back in the previous environment, it is not well suited to survive. The new strain is not something *more* than it was before. In actuality, it is something *less*—it is narrowly specialized to survive in a new environment while being less capable of surviving in the previous environment. It is well suited for the new but no longer suited to the old. There needs to be a gain of DNA information to change from one species to another. Mutation does not lead to a gain in DNA. There is no evidence of blind, unthinking nature causing an increase in DNA through mutation to cause an organism to develop into something it is not genetically designed to be, namely a new species or organism. Indeed, theistic evolutionists argue that God could guide the evolution and provide the additional DNA, but we have no evidence of his doing so.

3. The real story of the fossil record: The fossil record does not decisively indicate or prove macroevolution. Consistently, the fossil record shows a rapid existence (or coming into being or coming on the scene) of many species, mutations and microchanges within those species, and then the death or extinction of species. The fossil record does not show gradual development of species. Fossils reveal only morphological aspects of past animals (their shape or form), and we cannot prove derivation from similarity. Just because a more developed thing looks similar to a lesser developed thing does not necessarily mean the former came from the latter. For example, a pot looks like a highly developed spoon, but we know the spoon did not morph over time into a pot. Also, it is merely a guessing game to take fossilized bones from different creatures that look similar or related and then argue there is a progressive relationship between them. Too many unsubstantiated assumptions inform such a methodology. Moreover, to really understand the microbiological makeup of an animal, we need to analyze the soft tissue, because only cellular markings and other microbiological elements of soft tissue can tell us if there has been evolutionary development or relationship between organisms. The fossil record does not give us this microbiological material to study.

4. Cyclical changes within a species: When we observe mutation and microevolution in nature, we see cyclical changes within a species group. We do not see creatures developing into new creatures. Rather, animals shift or change back and forth within a limited range as determined by the DNA of the animal. They are still the same animal type. The morphological change in Darwin's finch case study is a good

example. The finches never developed into a new non-finch creature. Rather, there were changes in the size of the finch beak within a limited range, all determined by the genetic makeup of the finch. These changes were merely microevolutionary changes brought about by natural selection and limited by the DNA of the finch. This evidence of microevolution speaks only to the issue of microevolution and cannot be extrapolated to argue in favor of macroevolution, in which creatures change into new and different other creatures.

5. The challenge of irreducible complexity: The existence of irreducibly complex systems within organisms is a real problem for evolutionary models. Michael Behe has studied and continues to study irreducible systems in organisms, and his research continues to provide staggering challenges to macroevolutionary models. An irreducibly complex system is one that requires all of the parts to be simultaneously fully formed, arranged in the proper order, and each part fully and properly functioning in the system. Intelligent design research continues to uncover all kinds of irreducibly complex systems within organisms, like DNA, various biological "machines" within the cell, the cell wall, cilia on bacteria, vision or sight systems, and blood clotting mechanisms, just to name a few. Living systems are irreducibly complex, and the existence of the multitude of irreducibly complex systems within a single organism, let alone all of the diversity of life itself, simply cannot be explained by natural selection and macroevolution.

This issue of irreducible complexity is such a serious challenge to macroevolutionary theories that evolutionists continue to attack it as an argument for intelligent design. However, their critiques are unsuccessful. For example, Behe has used the basic mousetrap as an illustration of an irreducibly complex system. Evolutionists came up with a simpler mousetrap to argue that the mousetrap was not irreducibly complex and thus claimed Behe's argument falls apart. The problem for the evolutionist in this counter-example is that it took an intelligent person to design the new, simpler (yet still irreducibly complex) mousetrap, which argues in favor of Behe's theory rather than against it. Another strategy for countering some intelligent design theories is to make up unproven possible explanations. For example, some evolutionists have theorized that there must be biochemical scaffolds around an irreducibly complex molecular system that allow it to evolve. The problem here is that there is no evidence for these scaffolds and, if they do exist, what is the explanation of their origin and irreducible complexity? I encourage you to read more about the challenges that irreducible complexity raises against macroevolutionary models (see the reading list provided in the previous exchange).

6. Nonviable transitional organisms: Another significant problem with macroevolutionary models is the issue of the nonviability of transitional organisms. Let's say, for the sake of argument, that a creature possessing wing-like appendages with scales is morphing somehow into a creature with feathers. Let's put aside the question of where the new DNA comes from that allows the creature to grow feathers. Let's just assume a creature that has scales is somehow starting to grow feathers. Well, this change must happen gradually (according to Darwinian macroevolutionary theory). At some point, the creature no longer has the protective scales that allowed it to survive in its environment. It hasn't developed proper wings just yet and can't fly away from its predators, and it probably now would have more predators than before since it now lacks its scaly defenses. Since macroevolution is unguided and random, there is no telling if and when any other changes may or may not take place to help the transitional creature survive. As it is transforming, this creature becomes increasingly vulnerable and eventually nonviable.

Consider another example: there is a huge difference between the avian and reptilian heart. Yet, if birds eventually evolved from reptiles, the heart had to change significantly. Depending upon which part of the reptile was evolving first into the bird (again, such macroevolutionary changes are random and unguided, so we cannot assume all the necessary changes occur simultaneously), at some point, the heart would not be appropriate for the organism and would not function properly to keep it alive. Consider, too, that all living creatures are irreducibly complex, and for a transitional organism to survive, hundreds if not thousands of morphological, neurological, cellular, and other changes would have to occur, nearly simultaneously. It just isn't reasonable to believe that such changes occur gradually in an unguided way; not to mention that the fossil record simply does not provide us with uncontested, unambiguous evidence of transitional animals. (Yes, there are a few fragmentary fossils that evolutionists claim to be examples of transitional animals, but they are by no means conclusive nor is there consensus regarding the transitional nature of these fossil remains.)

As I continue to study evolutionary models and to consider the challenges raised by intelligent design scientists, I find that the evolutionary science is much too flawed by evidentiary and logical problems to justify macroevolution as a correct theory for the origin and diversity of life on the planet. Too much scientific evidence argues against macroevolution, and too much scientific evidence argues for intelligent design. Please do not make the same mistake committed by many in the press and by many opponents of intelligent design: intelligent design is not the same as creationism, all intelligent design scientists are not necessarily theists (there are many atheists and agnostics who concede the explanatory power of intelligent design theory and science), and all intelligent design proponents do not necessarily believe in theistic creation (many acknowledge that the evidence points to design, but they do not know the ultimate causation of that design). The critiques of macroevolution leveled by intelligent design scientists are not religious or theological or metaphysical objections; rather, they are scientific criticisms. That said, it is my informed opinion that theistic creation is the best explanation for the intelligent design we see in the universe, on the planet (ecological systems), and in biological life. Of course, I could be wrong. But, and here I'm using the same principle used by all scientists (known as the argument from the best explanation), I believe that given the evidence thus far, the best explanation for the complex design of the universe and of life itself lies in theistic creation.

I hope this helps answer your question. Again, I recommend reading through the sources I listed in our previous e-mail exchange. Study the evidence and the work of these scientists and theorists, and I think you'll agree that intelligent design and theistic creation as an explanation for the design we see in the universe and in biological life are not simply God-of-the-gaps explanations.

Cheers,
Prof. Dave

Exchange 6

I'm Having Some Problems Accepting the Cain Narrative in Genesis

Dear Prof,

It's been a little while since we've chatted about religion, faith, and belief, but our discussions have been on my mind. You have given me a lot of scientific information to help sustain a reasonable faith in theism, and I want to explore Christian theism more carefully. So, I decided to take you up on your suggestion to start reading the Bible for myself. I agree that it really isn't fair or intellectually honest to critique the Bible and the claims of biblical Christianity if I've never read the Bible. So, I'm giving it a try. I must confess: it's more challenging than I was expecting. As I read through Genesis, some questions came to mind:

1. Who was Cain afraid of when he became a restless wanderer of the Earth? It seems the only people alive at that point were Adam and Eve, yet God put a mark on Cain so that no one who found him would harm him; otherwise, they would suffer vengeance seven times over or something like that. Where did these supposed other people come from?

2. Who was Cain's wife and where did she come from? The Bible clearly says Adam and Eve had Cain and Abel, but nothing is said of any females. The Bible mentions the birth of Seth, but this third child was mentioned after Cain was banished, married, and began creating a city and lineages of his own. I'm confused.

3. If Adam and Eve did have other children, specifically females, why doesn't the Bible say so? It seems important for the sake of complete lineages and for the sake of explaining who came from where in the beginning of time. And certainly it seems important to list all the names for the sake of consistency in writing. The Bible seems to mention every name in the lineage of Cain, yet it doesn't say who Cain was afraid of or where his wife, the woman who bore all these children, came from. I understand that the men's names were important for tracing lineages, but you need a woman to even make a man, unless you are God creating stuff out of nothing all over the place. It only seems logical and would make for consistent and parallel writing to include the women's names as well. Or, at least tell us who the father was of these people Cain was afraid of when he was cast out into Nod, and whether those people he was afraid of had baby girls (if, for example, Cain's wife was not his sister, born of Adam and Eve).

I guess the thrust of my questions is the same for all of them, and that is: where did all these other people come from?

One thing I did notice, which could explain all of this, is that women seem to be omitted altogether from these early verses, with the exception of Eve (I noticed that even the names Adam and Eve are mentioned very seldom and instead they are often called "the man" and "the woman"). For example, when the Bible describes Cain's lineages, there is not one woman's name mentioned (though it does say that Cain had a wife, and that one of Cain's male descendants had two wives), which leads me to believe that Adam and Eve could have had baby girls; they just weren't mentioned for whatever reason. But am I just "reading into" the Bible, which is problematic? (Could I also get a quick review on that issue of "reading into" and "reading out of" the Bible, by the way? I remember you saying something in one of our other conversations about how we have to be careful in our strategies for interpreting the Bible.)

So to recap: why weren't the girls born of Adam and Eve mentioned if they existed? Why mention Cain's wife and the two wives of one of his descendants but not mention the daughters of Adam and Eve?

Sincerely,
Seeker

Dear Seeker,

As always, you have good and important questions. Many skeptics raise these same questions as a way to point out deficiencies in Scripture and to suggest the Bible is not to be believed because it is contradictory or does not make sense or cannot account for apparent gaps in its own creation account. First, God did not reveal all things to the Scripture writers, only that which he deemed necessary and important to learn about various spiritual truths and to provide the necessary information regarding his plan of salvation, culminating in Jesus Christ. Remember, we are limited beings and cannot have complete knowledge, but God reveals enough to us in the Bible to give us sufficient knowledge to come to faith in him and his plan of salvation through Jesus Christ. Also, this issue of Adam and Eve's children and the wives for Cain and the other male offspring is not a complication, gap, or inconsistency in Scripture. The existence of the women and other children is accounted for; it's just easy to miss if we are not reading carefully.

According to the biblical account, Adam and Eve are the parents of all humans to this day (Gen 3:20)—biblical common ancestors, if you will. This is important to know so that we can remember that all human beings of all races are equal, that all human beings are born in sin (from Adam and Eve who first sinned), and that all humans are thus in need of salvation (Paul in his letter to the Romans in the New Testament makes this point clear, and understanding Paul's message in Romans depends upon our understanding of the Genesis account). The second Adam—Christ—came to take the penalty of human sin upon himself, to be punished in our place, and this gift of God's grace is available to all human beings who believe, because all people come from the first Adam and can be redeemed by faith in the second Adam (Christ). No human being is left out of this plan of salvation, and salvation is extended to all human beings of all races of all nations who believe in Christ. This grace must be received by faith.

Through Scripture, God did not reveal all the genealogies of all the human beings. Rather, he revealed those lines that lead from the first Adam, through the patriarchs, to David, and then to Jesus. This is the genealogy of God's plan of salvation. This genealogy is more important than knowing all the parents of all the humans. Lineage is traditionally recorded through the fathers, so that is why these genealogies emphasize fathers, though mothers are not left out entirely, as you can see if you study the other biblical genealogies as well. This is not to suggest that women are viewed as unimportant by Scripture—that would be an inaccurate, agenda-driven "reading into" Scripture that results in a false understanding. Ancient Near-Eastern cultures were patriarchal, but this does not automatically or by necessity mean that these cultures were therefore anti-women.

Cain's wife's name is not mentioned, but it is logical from Scripture to deduce that she was his sister born from Adam and Eve. Genesis chapter 5, verse 4, records that Adam lived 930 years and had sons and daughters (so, the Bible does mention sons and daughters of Adam and Eve, just not all of them by name). You can have a lot of sons and daughters in that time frame. Indeed, many people today find it hard to believe that humans could live such long periods of time; however, it is not an illogical claim. If God originally created humans in a pure and sinless state as described in Genesis, then it is reasonable to conclude that these first humans were physically purer and more genetically rich than we are today, and because of disease and mutation entering into the human condition via the fall into sin, it makes sense that humans would, over time, become more and more impure, more diseased, and thus live shorter lives now than in the very beginning. Since humans were more genetically pure during the time of Adam and Eve and lived longer lives, we can understand how populations grew and how different people groups developed into various cultures and religions over time as they moved further and further away from the revealed truth of God. So, Cain's wife was one of his many sisters that Adam and Eve had during their hundreds of years of procreating.

But, if Cain married his sister, doesn't that mean he violated the incest taboo? No, because incest was not a necessary taboo until much later. It is logical to conclude, based upon what we know of genetics, that the further we go back in genetic history, the more information-rich and diverse the gene pool (even though there were fewer people as we go back in history, each person's DNA was informationally rich and diverse). In other words, it is reasonable to maintain that Adam and Eve contained all the genetic information of all the possible human people groups or races that were to develop later. Thus, it was not biologically problematic for Adam and Eve's children to intermarry and to procreate. However, as the gene pool thinned out, so to speak, or became more narrow and specialized, it became necessary to worry about the negative ramifications of inbreeding; thus, incest eventually and rightfully became taboo.

Notice, too, that in the account of Cain's murder of Abel and the resulting banishment described in Genesis chapter 4, God and Cain speak in the future tense when discussing his curse—they are anticipating what will eventually happen to him once cities develop and the inhabitants learn about Cain and what he did. Time frames are not given in this passage, so we don't know how much time has passed since the birth of Cain and his murder of Abel, and we don't know how much time passed between when he was banished and when he later found his wife. It could be that some of the numerous offspring of Adam and Eve were forming towns or cities, and Cain feared these people, or he could be anticipating the necessity to fear the people who would eventually exist and learn of his treachery, as that horrendous crime of fratricide would be carried along as part of the cultural narratives of these early communities.

So, to answer your main question: all the people mentioned or alluded to came from Adam and Eve, who were having children for several hundred years.

Indeed, we have to be careful not to "read into" Scripture, and instead we should "read out" of Scripture what it is intending to communicate. It is important to note that intent is prior to content, and sometimes we take certain preconceived notions, prejudices, assumptions, and principles into the text and thus subjectively determine what we want it to mean. Our intentions determine the content of our interpretation. We must be aware of our preconceptions and strive to allow the meaning to come out clearly from the text. Meaning is what the authors of Scripture (as inspired by God) intended to say. It is not always easy to know this meaning, but we can do our best to allow the plain language of the text to guide our understanding of meaning. Also, the more we learn about the original historical and cultural contexts of the events being described and the context of the scriptural message (the purpose of that particular book or passage in relation to other passages in the Bible), the better able we are to understand the meaning.

The significance of a passage is basically how we can apply the passage to our lives. But, we must not confuse meaning with significance.

When we "read into" the text what we want it to mean based upon our own preconceptions, then we are not accurately interpreting the passage and we misconstrue its meaning. What I described above regarding Adam and Eve and their offspring is not reading into Scripture what I want it to say just to fit my preconceived notions. Rather, based upon the evidence given in Scripture and the scientific knowledge we have of genetics, we can make a reasonable deduction that is consistent with Scripture and that does not twist Scripture into meaning something it clearly does not intend to mean.

Hope this helps. Keep reading and thinking!

Cheers,
Prof. Dave

Exchange 7

Why Are There Genealogies in the Bible and Can They Be Used to Date the Earth?

Dear Prof,

Your explanation of *meaning* and *significance* was very helpful, and I agree that it is important to distinguish between interpretation (what God, through the biblical writers, is saying) and application (how we apply biblical meaning to our lives). I'm trying to keep these ideas in mind as I continue to read Genesis and as I think about some ideas I've heard and read about. For example, I know that some people point to the genealogies in the Bible, particularly those in Genesis, as proof that the earth is very young. Yet, there is so much evidence from the scientific community that suggests the earth and the universe are very old. Are faith in science and faith in the Bible incompatible? Does the Bible really prove that the earth and the universe are young? Does science really prove that the universe is old? Can biblical genealogies be used to date the earth? I'm really struggling with these questions, and I'm wondering to what extent are some people "reading into" the Bible certain ideas about science that are not reasonable. To be fair, I'm also wondering about some claims of scientists and those who have faith in science: namely, are their negative claims about the Bible and Christianity fair and reasonable?

I'm continuing to read through Genesis and the Old Testament, and I look forward to your response when you get a chance. I know you are very busy and in the midst of grading papers—don't be too hard on your students. Ha ha!

Sincerely,
Seeker

Dear Seeker,

I'm so glad to hear you are continuing to read Genesis and the Old Testament. Some sections may be tough going, but hang in there, and I'll try to answer your questions as they come up. Thanks for thinking about my students! I'm taking a break from grading some research papers from my science fiction class. My students are doing very well, and that makes me happy. Actually, my mind is in science discourse mode, so it's a great time to address some of your questions about science and the Bible.

The heart of your questions regarding genealogies is huge. The study of biblical genealogies is a whole subspecialty of scriptural analysis and biblical hermeneutics (study of interpretation), and to be honest, I'm still learning about this branch of theological scholarship. I'll share with you what I understand at this point in my own study of this topic. To start, we have to remember that while the Bible is historical and contains historical writings (among other genres such as philosophy, poetry, wisdom literature, theology, letters, and eyewitness narrative), its main purpose is not to provide a succinct way to date the age of the earth. Now, that is not to say that we cannot derive some understanding of the age of the earth from the Bible, but we must be careful when doing so, for earth-dating is not an exact science. Mainly, the Bible reveals God's character, his nature, his creative acts, his relationship with his creation, his plans and purposes for his creation, and his historical plan of salvation through Christ. The genealogies found in the Bible speak primarily to this later purpose: the lineage of the first Adam through to Abraham, God's covenant with Abraham to bring forth God's people through whom God provides the Messiah, and the messianic lineage through "the root of Jesse" or King David to, ultimately, Christ, the "Second Adam."

Genealogies serve a domestic, political, and religious function. They establish family lines and rights of inheritance (domestic), establish rights and lineage of kings (political), and determine the priestly lineage (religious). The main function of the genealogies in the Bible is threefold:

1. To reveal the family of God through Christ (all who believe in Christ become true children of God and share in the inheritance of the Son of God).

2. To establish the divine kingship of Christ (the Messiah is the triumphant king who will return in glory as revealed in Revelation).

3. To establish Christ as the final and ultimate priest. The Messiah, Christ, is at once the Son of God (family), the Divine King (political), and the High Priest (religious), and the genealogies primarily serve to reveal this nature of Christ as the Savior for all who believe in him.

Many scholars suggest that there may be some gaps or missing generations in the genealogies of Genesis chapters 5 and 11 (note that these gaps can be at most a few thousand years). Also, the precise chronological dating within the books of Kings and Chronicles is not fully understood in exact contemporary terms, because dating systems and calendars were different in the ancient Near East, and different civilizations recorded their own history and that of their neighboring cultures differently. So, it is challenging to get an exact figure from the Bible when it comes to dating the age of civilizations, let alone the age of the earth. Also, where the ages of individuals within the genealogical lists are not specifically mentioned, we can at best make educated guesses and assumptions. What this means is that we cannot get an exact date from biblical history. However, comparing what many Bible scholars (past and present) have calculated based upon a scholarly analysis of genealogies and chronologies with other historical records from the ancient Near East, biblical creationists who hold to a young earth argue that the earth is anywhere from 6,000 to 12,000 years old. A good book that goes into much more detail about genealogies, chronologies, and the age of the earth is *The Genesis Record: A Scientific and Devotional Commentary on the Book of Beginnings*, by Henry M. Morris. This book is a very detailed exposition of the book of Genesis.

Regarding the genealogy of Christ in Matthew and Luke in the New Testament: many skeptics try to say that these are contradictory genealogies and thus suggest there are errors in Scripture. Upon closer (and proper) analysis, what we see is that these two different writers reveal the lineage of Christ in two different ways: Matthew traces the legal lineage of Christ to Abraham through Joseph, the legal (adoptive) father (Matthew 1:1–17), while Luke traces the lineage of Christ through Mary to Abraham and then through to Adam (Luke 3:23–38). These two genealogical lists for Christ are complementary, not contradictory, and thus collectively point to Christ's unique fulfillment of Old Testament prophecy concerning the Messiah.

Now, as to your other questions regarding the age of the universe and the relationship(s) between faith in science and faith in the Bible, I must admit that I sometimes also struggle with this. To deny my struggle would be intellectually and spiritually dishonest. I, too, grapple with what amounts to overwhelming scientific evidence that the universe is old. However, when I study and reflect upon this matter in detail, I realize some interesting points:

1. Few Western scholars in both theological and "scientific" circles doubted a young age of the universe and the earth before the eighteenth century and into the nineteenth century (I put *scientific* in quotes here because the terms *science* and *scientist* were not common terms until roughly the nineteenth century. Before then, the term "natural philosophy" was more commonly used). Scientists up to this point started with the intellectually honest and healthy view that we live in a fallen created order and that we are fallen creatures examining a fallen world. As such, we must be careful what conclusions we make from observing a fallen world, for the conclusions themselves may not be fully accurate. This is a crucial point.

2. Once the so-called enlightenment in the eighteenth century sought to replace God with man and to dismiss all revealed religions and theology ("God talk") as irrational, then secular scientists viewed themselves (the mere human) as the presuppositional focus of truth. They decided that the only thing that could be empirically studied was the natural world and the only conclusions accepted were naturalistic ones. This methodology determines the types of questions scientists ask (and don't ask) and prescribes the types of answers accepted (and rejected). The clear result of this naturalistic presupposition is that there can be no supernatural causes and no intelligent causes in a naturalistic process. There can only be unguided, unintelligent, random forces acting in nature.

   Of course, this methodology completely ignores the question of how nature even got here to begin with, and it cannot answer the basic question of why there is anything here at all. Rejecting the possibility of a supernatural or intelligent cause to the universe necessitates that everything be explained by natural causes. Noting that natural processes take a long time to do anything, it is only logical to conclude that it will take immense amounts of time to cause more complex things to exist (assuming to begin with that unguided, unintelligent natural forces can even cause complexity to come from noncomplexity or more complex systems to develop on their own from less complex systems). Therefore, naturalistic approaches to answering the question of origins must assume a really old universe (or assume the steady-state, eternal, always existing universe, which we know scientifically is so highly improbable as to be impossible). Also, to argue that life developed naturalistically all by itself, one must assume that the earth must be really, really old. You see how the naturalistic presuppositions necessitate an old universe and an old earth? Therefore, no matter what evidence is presented, the methodological naturalist (one who assumes that the material is all that exists and who accepts only natural causes as explanations for observed effects) will not accept anything other than an old universe and an old earth.

3. Science is not truth, nor is science the only arbiter of truth. Science can help us discover and know truth, but it is not the last say on what is truth. Naturalistic science has serious limitations. The science is only as good as its presuppositions, and it can only reveal that which fits into its presuppositions. So, we must examine the presuppositions. Science limited by naturalism is necessarily limited. Science that allows for both naturalism and supernaturalism is less limited. Two really good books that examine these issues are J. P. Moreland's *The Creation Hypothesis* and Cornelius G. Hunter's *Science's Blind Spot*.

4. There are well-intentioned Christians who try to resolve the differences between secular science and biblical truth. For example, Hugh Ross is a leading astrophysicist who argues for an old universe and old earth while also arguing that this view is not incompatible with the Bible. He has written many excellent books, and a really good one that lays out his position with both scientific and biblical evidences is *A Matter of Days: Resolving a Creation Controversy*. Ross is a committed Christian and successful scientist, yet other Christian thinkers note that in some of his conclusions he privileges naturalistic science over the Bible. Why is this a problem? These other thinkers state that if, as a Christian, one believes the Bible to be the inspired word of God, then one should never try to mold the Bible to man's knowledge

but, rather, come to understand man's knowledge in the context of God's revealed knowledge in the Scriptures. Some Christian critics of Ross (and other Christian theists who believe what Ross advocates) argue that the result of Ross's (and other's) attempts to reconcile secular science with the Biblical record is unbiblical theology. These critics argue that because Ross accepts an old earth he then has to come up with a set of unbiblical explanations as to why there are death and disease before sin. (The Bible states that death and disease entered the world after humans sinned; but the old earth model reveals death and disease before humans ever existed.) These Christian critics note that Ross and other theistic evolutionists (those who believe that God used macroevolutionary processes to create the diversity of life on earth) seem to accept the knowledge generated by man as true and then must twist what God has said in his word to make it fit what man is saying. The critics note that it could be the finite men who have it wrong and that what the infinite God revealed in his Word is correct. If one must choose which set of ideas to privilege, these critics argue, one should privilege God's ideas over human ideas. On the other hand, Ross and others holding to his views argue that they are not privileging human thought over God's revealed truth but, rather, see both as complementary and pointing to the same truth.

5. The debate for Christians comes down to how best to interpret Scripture. One issue some biblical scholars note is that many theistic evolutionists (like Hugh Ross) are great scientists, but they are not good Hebrew scholars. Therefore, it is possible that they make incorrect statements about what the original Hebrew, the language of the Old Testament, means. The theistic evolutionists' arguments sound convincing if we accept their interpretation of the Hebrew texts. However, many critics point out that their Hebrew is quite faulty. One such vocal critic is Dr. Jonathan Sarfati, who is a renowned chemist (PhD in physical chemistry) and also a Hebrew scholar. He has written a book called *Refuting Compromise*, which is a direct refutation of the science and biblical interpretation proposed by Ross. Note: This is an ongoing debate within the Christian community, and it is far from being resolved. My suggestion is to not let this debate distract you from what is of primary importance: who is Jesus Christ and what does he mean to you, your life, and your ultimate destiny?

Is there evidence to support the old universe and old earth? Yes. Is there evidence to support the young universe and the young earth? Yes. Both camps are examining the exact same artifacts. But, the secularists and naturalists are limited in their approach and the types of conclusions they are willing to accept. The theistic scientists are also not neutral, but I believe they are more open-minded. One does not have to be neutral in order to be open-minded. The theist is more willing to examine a wider range of evidence and facts and to consider a wider range of possible explanations and conclusions than the secular naturalist.

I am not a scientist. However, when I look at what the various scientists are saying, I find that there is some compelling evidence for a young earth and plenty of evidence for an old earth. I have concluded (but am still learning and investigating) that when there are such unresolved questions, I must turn to God, not to man. However, I recognize that man has a finite mind whereas God has an infinite mind, and it is possible that the finite man does not properly understand some things God has revealed in Scripture or that some are misreading the Bible to fit their presuppositions. A similar interpretive problem can exist in science. Some science may be pointing to an old earth and universe, but I recognize that some of this science could be wrong. Similarly, some science may be pointing to a young earth, and this science may have it wrong too. This does not make me antiscience. Rather, it makes me anti–secular humanism. That is, I reject the presupposition that man is the center of knowledge and that he is all we can rely upon for our understanding of truth. My position is not irrational. In fact, it is the height of rationality. Also, I do not believe that science is taboo per se. Science is but a tool and a mode of knowledge discovery (epistemology). I believe that God gave us the capacity to develop science so as to better understand the reality he made and into which he placed us. So, as such, science is not blasphemous. The way it is used can be blasphemous, like trying to use science to force an antitheistic agenda. (Similarly, some scholars can use theology for blasphemous ends.) But this reality does not cause me to reject science (just as misuses of theology do not cause me to reject theology). It causes me instead to reject the ideas of the person trying to use science (or theology) for such a misguided agenda.

Wow, this message is longer than I was expecting it to be, but I hope it helps. I had better get back to grading my SF papers.

Cheers,
Prof. Dave

Exchange 8

Isn't the Bible Just a Bunch of Tales Compiled by Men to Achieve Their Subjective Agenda?

Dear Prof,

How's it going? Sorry I haven't e-mailed you in a while, but I've been really busy. But don't worry, I'm still reading through the Bible. I must say, it's more of a challenge than I was expecting, and I'm not quite sure what to make of it all. I'm confused in spots, but I'm sticking with it. One thing I wasn't expecting was for there to be so many different books by so many different writers, spread out over such long periods of time. Now I'm starting to wonder about why we have the books that we have in the Bible. I mean, who's to say these are the right books? How do we know that a few men just didn't get together and subjectively decide what should and should not be in the Bible, just to suit their own personal or political agenda? I've seen some shows on the Discovery Channel that seem to be suggesting that the Bible really doesn't include the whole story and that a lot has been left out due to later religious leaders stacking the deck in their favor, so to speak. I don't know if this is true or not, but it makes some sense to me, and I wouldn't be surprised if it were true. Do you know anything about this issue? Hope to hear from you soon.

Sincerely,
Seeker

Dear Seeker,

It's so good to hear from you. I was afraid that maybe my last e-mail was just too much and you were calling it quits. I'm glad to know you are sticking with it. I've been pretty busy too, but your e-mail comes at a very good time. My semester is finished and I've submitted all of my grades. I have a few weeks to relax before my next semester begins. So, I'll do my best to answer your questions.

What you are asking is generally known as canon formation, or the process by which certain books of the Bible were considered Holy Scripture. This is a very complex topic, and I will do my best to summarize some of the key issues for you. I encourage you to study further by following up with the books listed at the end of this message. (These are the resources I used when studying these issues and compiling the information that follows.)

I. HOW DID WE GET THE BIBLE?—THE CANON?

The word *canon* comes from the Greek *kanon*, which literally means *reed*. A reed was commonly used as a measuring stick, so canon simply refers to the rule or criteria by which we measure something. The biblical canon is the official, accepted list of books that have passed a godly measure or standard. Please note that, contrary to what is commonly stated in the popular media, the church and the church fathers did not determine or create the canon or the Bible; that is, they did not determine which books are the inspired word of God. Rather, they *recognized* God's inspiration and *discovered* which writings are truly Scripture. How did they recognize and discover what ought to be included in the canon? Here are the key tests for canonicity or inclusion in the canon:

1. Was the book written by a prophet of God or a person accredited of God? Indeed, we don't know who wrote some of the books of the Bible; however, just because we don't know exactly who wrote a particular book doesn't mean this person is not a prophet of God—we can tell by what he says, how he says it, and how what is written coheres with other passages of Scripture.

2. Was the writer confirmed by acts of God (miracles or a sign to confirm the prophetic nature of the writer)?

3. Did the message tell the truth about God and his nature (not contradictory elements or characteristics)? (See for example 2 Corinthians 1:17–18; Hebrews 6:18.)

4. Does the message come with the power of God (that is, the transforming and edifying power of God)? (See for example, Hebrews 4:12; 2 Timothy 3:16–17; 1 Peter 1:23.)

5. Was it accepted by the people of God? (See for example 1 Thessalonians 2:13 [here, Paul's writings are received as the word of God]; 2 Peter 3:15b–16 [here, Paul's letters are viewed by Peter as equivalent with Old Testament Scripture].)

When the biblical canon was taking shape, godly men of the faith prayerfully and carefully considered the various writings and measured them according to these standards, and these men were able to recognize which books were canonical and which were not. They did not simply pick and choose based upon their own subjective personal agendas or political interests.

II. THE OLD TESTAMENT CANON

A Brief History

The Jewish canon was established by the fourth century BC and certainly no later than 150 BC. The Jews believed that God had ceased to speak directly to his people by the fourth century BC, and thus the Jewish Bible (what Christians refer to as the Old Testament) does not contain any works written after this point. Note that the Old Testament adhered to by Protestant Christians is the same as the traditional Jewish Bible (the books are merely arranged differently).

Apocrypha

This word is from the Greek, *apokruphos*, which means *hidden* or *concealed*. The apocrypha are Jewish writings from 300 BC to 200 AD, written after the time when the Jews believed God had stopped speaking to his people through prophetic utterances, and are thus not considered to be Scripture or the inspired word of God by Jews or Protestant Christians. Some Jews and Christians refer to these texts as learned or important writings, but not as the inspired word of God. Note that these texts were not considered to be Holy Scripture by Jews and all Christians through the 1500s AD. However, the Roman Catholic Church later accepted the apocrypha as canonical at the Trent Council (1545–63 AD), mainly in a political move against Martin Luther and the Protestant Reformation (this council was formed primarily in reaction against the Reformation). The books of the apocrypha include: 1 and 2 Esdras, Tobit, Judith, additions to Esther, The Wisdom of Solomon, The Wisdom of Sirach, Baruch, Bel and the Dragon, The Song of the Three Hebrew Children, The Prayer of Manasseh, and 1 and 2 Maccabees.

Accepted Books of the Old Testament

The Traditional Jewish grouping of the accepted books is as follows:

1. The Law of Moses: Genesis, Exodus, Leviticus, Numbers, Deuteronomy

2. The Prophets: Joshua, Judges, Samuel, Kings, Isaiah, Jeremiah, Ezekiel, The Twelve (Latter Prophets)

3. The Writings (poetical books, wisdom, and historical books): Psalms, Proverbs, Job, Song of Songs, Ruth, Lamentations, Esther, Ecclesiastes, Daniel, Ezra-Nehemiah, Chronicles

Christians accept these books as canonical for the following reasons:

1. They pass the tests for divine Scripture (see above).

2. They are accepted by Jewish tradition. (Who are we to tell the Jews what should or should not be in their traditional canon?)

3. Philo (20 BC–40AD), a Jewish philosopher, and Josephus (30–100 AD), a Jewish historian, both quote extensively from the traditional Old Testament and do not include any apocryphal books as part of Scripture.

4. Christ and the apostles attested to their authenticity as Scripture.

5. Christ and the apostles never cite any apocryphal book as Scripture. They knew of them and made allusion to them, but never presented them as Scripture.

6. During Jesus' time, the Old Testament was referred to as "the law and prophets" (see for example Matthew 5:17; Luke 24:27), meaning all of the Old Testament as we know it, without the apocrypha.

7. Christ taught only from the traditional Scripture. (See for example Matthew 23:35; Luke 11: 50–51; Luke 24:44. These references span from Genesis to Second Chronicles, which in the Hebrew arrangement is the last book of the Old Testament. The point here is that Christ affirmed that all of the writings of the traditional Old Testament, from beginning to end, are the inspired word of God, all attesting to and pointing to himself.)

III. THE NEW TESTAMENT CANON

The Gospels and the Letters Were Originally Written between 30 AD and 100 AD

The Gospels were written to record the life, miracles, teachings, and divinity of Christ. They provide narrative proof and historical evidence for Christ and his teachings. These early texts were used to spread the knowledge of God's salvation plan, to maintain the integrity of the early church, and to provide instruction for how to live for Christ. Furthermore, these early and original texts were used to correct false teachings that were later introduced to compete with the true Gospel of Christ as recorded by the apostles and eyewitness accounts.

Brief History of Why These Books Were Originally Collected between 140 AD and 400 AD

These books were written by an apostle or prophet of God or by a trustworthy compiler of eyewitness information (as in the case of Luke's writings) and thus understood to be authoritative and important. They were used to instruct the early church, which needed authoritative scriptures to explain and clarify the teachings of Christ. These New Testament books were also used to refute the rise of church heretics, as early as 140 AD. A heretical teaching was simply a point of view that differed from what was taught by Christ and his apostles as recorded by the apostles and eyewitnesses to Christ. The books of the New Testament were further used to counter and correct counterfeit books read by the early church. Finally, these New Testament books were the texts used in missions to spread the teachings of Christ to all the peoples of the known world at that time.

Apocrypha and Gnostic Gospels

These other books were written in the early first century (65 AD–170 AD) and as late as the fourth century AD. They are texts written by various writers and teachers of the early church that introduced false doctrines or teachings that contradicted the original teachings of Christ as recorded by his apostles and eyewitnesses. Such books were rejected early on as noncanonical. Indeed, some of these noncanonical books were recognized locally (in limited regions) and temporarily (for a very short period of time) by only a few people; no major canon or church council ever included them as inspired books of the Bible. Some of these apocryphal books include: Epistle of Pseudo-Barnabas; Shepherd of Hermas; Didache, Teaching of the Twelve; Apocalypse of Peter; Epistle to the Laodiceans; The Seven Epistles of Ignatius; The Gospel of Thomas; The Secret Book of James; The Gospel of Mary; The Acts of Peter; The Acts of Thomas; and The Gospel of the Savior.

The Accepted Books of the New Testament

The canonical Gospels and letters were originally written in the first century AD (all before 100 AD) and were formally accepted and organized into the New Testament by the fourth century AD. By the early second century (100–120 AD) the four Gospels (Matthew, Mark, Luke, and John) were already recognized as the only canonical and authoritative Gospels of Jesus Christ by such early church fathers as Polycarp, Justin Martyr, Ignatius, and Irenaeus. Moreover, twenty-four of the final twenty-seven accepted books of the New Testament were cited by Ignatius as early as 107 AD. As early as 110 AD, eighteen of the twenty-seven accepted books were cited by Polycarp. The complete New Testament was formally listed by Athanasius of Alexandria in 367 AD. Shortly thereafter, Jerome and Augustine confirmed this list of twenty-seven books as the only canonical New Testament books. This list was later reaffirmed by two church councils: the Synod of Hippo in 393 AD and the Third Synod of Carthage in 397 AD. This list has not been significantly challenged since these fourth-century councils.

Well, once again it seems I may have overwhelmed you with a lot of information. But, I want you to understand that there is specific historical information that addresses your very important questions, and I also want you to understand the importance of having reliable information. Much is reported in the popular media these days that simply is not correct, is incomplete, or that misrepresents the historical facts. I hope this e-mail helps point you in the right direction. I encourage you to dig deeper into these issues by reading such books as the following:

> Bruce, F. F. *The Books and Parchments: How We Got Our English Bible*. Old Tappan, NJ: Fleming H. Revell, 1984.
> ———. *The Canon of Scripture*. Downers Grove, IL: InterVarsity, 1988.
> Ewert, David. *From Ancient Tablets to Modern Translations: A General Introduction to the Bible*. Grand Rapids: Zondervan, 1983.
> McDowell, Josh. *The New Evidence that Demands a Verdict*. Nashville: Thomas Nelson, 1999.
> Metzger, Bruce M. *The Text of the New Testament*. New York: Oxford University Press, 1968.
> Geisler, Norman, and William E. Nix. *A General Introduction to the Bible*. Chicago: Moody, 1986.

I hope this helps a bit, and let me know if you have other questions.

Cheers,
Prof. Dave

Exchange 9

I Don't Know If I Can Trust the New Testament Record

Dear Prof,

Yikes! That was one of the longest e-mails I've ever received. There's a lot of information that I still have to chew over. But, reading your message did lead me to ask another question regarding the New Testament. I've heard some people say it's all fiction, others say the disciples of Jesus made it all up, and still others have said it is reliable history. Who's right here? To be honest, I don't think I can believe that the New Testament is real history. I hope you can shed some light on this one. (BTW, I'm bracing myself for another long message. Ha ha.)

Sincerely,
Seeker

Dear Seeker,

Yeah, that last e-mail was rather long. I kept telling myself it's too much as I was writing it, but there is just so much information to be shared. I do hope you will continue to review what I wrote and follow up with some of the readings I suggested at the end. You are asking the right questions, and I pray that my responses are helpful to you.

Well, your next question is just as big and important as your previous one. My response may again be longish, and I'll try to keep it brief. But, I make no guarantee. Indeed, many people try to dismiss the New Testament as mere fairy tale or religious fabrication, but the simple truth of the matter is that the New Testament is a complex collection of first-century writings that has various genres, history being a major one. Many people will insist that the New Testament is nothing but legend, myth, and lore—fantasy, if you will. I study, write about, and teach Gothic literature, Romantic literature, science fiction, and fantasy literature, so I have read and analyzed quite a bit of legend, lore, and myth. The New Testament documents do not read like mythology or fantasy. C. S. Lewis, the renowned literary scholar, writer of fable and myth, and Christian philosopher, commented that he did not see any resemblance between the structures, styles, and expressions of mythology and the writings of the New Testament, and he suggested that anyone who claims the New Testament is mythology based upon textual analysis simply reveals his or her own incompetence as a literary critic.

Indeed, the New Testament contains descriptions of some remarkable and supernatural events, but the mere presence of the remarkable does not automatically make the narrative fictional or mythological. The New Testament contains roughly twenty-seven different documents written by nine different individuals who were either eyewitnesses to the events being described or who were contemporaries of eyewitnesses and compiled their eyewitness testimony. The dominant literary styles of the New Testament include historical writing, personal narrative, eyewitness testimony, and epistolary writing (real letters written to real people). There is one book, the Book of Revelation written by the Apostle John, that approaches myth; however, it is inaccurate to characterize it as myth. Rather, it is properly understood as apocalyptic writing, which involves the revelation of truth as expressed in visionary images. Moreover, this book is self-consciously aware of its own status as apocalyptic writing, and the writer presents it to readers as visionary writing. This book is an historically accurate description of what a real human being saw in his dreams at a particular point in his life within world history. What we make of his visions is a different matter, but the writing itself is a real and accurate representation of his dreams. From a literary perspective, it is more correct to view the New Testament writings as historical documents rather than mythology.

A reasonable question to ask, then, is: can we trust these historical documents? Are the New Testament writings reliable documents, or have they been changed, corrupted, and revised to suit the narrow views of a few powerful religious men? This, I think, is the heart of your question too. Some biblical scholars today believe the latter, like Bart Ehrman, who recently published the book *Misquoting Jesus: The Story behind Who Changed the Bible and Why* (2005). Interestingly, this is a book written for a wide audience (lay persons or nontheologians), but it is basically a summary of one of his earlier books, *Orthodox Corruptions of Scripture* (1993), written for theologians and biblical scholars. Please note that many of Ehrman's claims in the earlier book have been challenged and refuted by several scholars and theologians, revealing his conclusions to be false. Yet in his new book, which is based upon the refuted conclusions of his previous book, he simply presents the same false conclusions as if they were unchallenged truths.[1] Ironically, the unsuspecting lay audience may accept Ehrman's views as "gospel" even as he seeks to debunk the historical claims of the New Testament Gospel writers. Similarly, such is the ethos informing the exciting (yet implausible) conspiracy theories of fictional works like *The Da Vinci Code* (2003). Now, *that* is great fantasy. However, without a fuller understanding of the various textual and historical facts surrounding the writing of the New Testament, many readers are apt to confuse fantasy with historical fact, and they come away believing a myth instead of the truth.

Let's consider some evidence that these recent scholars and fictions overlook, evidence that severely undermines their perspectives and conclusions. All established and reputable biblical scholars now agree that the original New Testament documents were written by eyewitnesses to the events or by contemporaries of the eyewitnesses who recorded their testimonies, and that the original documents were written down between 50 and 100 AD (although recent discoveries are suggesting even earlier dates). These documents were all written within the lifetimes of those who witnessed the teachings and actions of Jesus Christ. There is not enough time between the actual events and when these documents were written for them to be corrupted by legend or lore. The New Testament eyewitness testimonies were presented originally to contemporary readers who themselves were either eyewitnesses to the events or who could easily verify the claims made in the documents. Therefore, if anything was recorded incorrectly, those who witnessed the events were still alive to challenge the record. No such challenges were issued and the documents continued to circulate through the first-century community of believers as authentic.

We should also note that New Testament writers such as Luke, Paul, John, and Peter attested to the fact that they were presenting eyewitness accounts (either their own or those of others). Therefore, any of their narratives and claims, from the simple geographical or historical detail to the

---

1. For a review and analysis of Ehrman's book, see Wallace, "Gospel According to Bart."

more incredible descriptions of the miraculous, could be verified or challenged by their contemporary readers. For example, to verify the truthfulness of what was being proclaimed and taught about Jesus, Luke compiled eyewitness accounts and explained his methodology and purpose in the very beginning of his Gospel of Luke: "Inasmuch as many have undertaken to compile a narrative of the things that have been accomplished among us, just as those who from the beginning were eyewitnesses and ministers of the word have delivered them to us, it seemed good to me also, having followed all things closely for some time past, to write an orderly account for you, most excellent Theophilus, that you may have certainty concerning the things you have been taught" (Luke 1:1–4). The purpose of Luke's work was to verify the truthfulness of what was being taught and proclaimed.

After narrating the historical events of the crucifixion from his own eyewitness account, John inserts a statement emphasizing that he is describing what he himself had witnessed in order to verify the truthfulness of his statements: "He [John] who saw it has borne witness—his testimony is true, and he knows that he is telling the truth—that you also may believe" (John 19:35). Throughout his Gospel and his letters to the early church, John makes similar statements that what he is writing is based upon his own eyewitness experiences that can be confirmed by others and is thus true historical description, not mythological fantasy.

In his letter to the believers in Corinth, Paul writes, "For I delivered to you as of first importance what I also received: that Christ died for our sins in accordance with the Scriptures, that he was buried, that he was raised on the third day in accordance with the Scriptures, and that he appeared to Cephas [Peter], then to the twelve. Then he appeared to more than five hundred brothers at one time, most of whom are still alive, though some have fallen asleep. Then he appeared to James, then to all the apostles. Last of all, as to one untimely born, he appeared also to me" (1 Cor 15:3–8). James, Peter, the original twelve (except Judas), and most of the 500 others were still alive when Paul made this statement, and his readers could have verified his claims by questioning these eyewitnesses.

Finally, Peter writes in one of his letters to the believers who were spread throughout Asia Minor, "For we did not follow cleverly devised myths when we made known to you the power and coming of our Lord Jesus Christ, but we were eyewitnesses of his majesty" (2 Peter 1:16). He makes it a point to distinguish his eyewitness accounts from fanciful tales or myths (i.e., the noneyewitness teachings that would be later developed in gnosticism), reminding them that his testimony could be corroborated or challenged by comparison to other eyewitness accounts. It does not seem reasonable that these New Testament writers would make such bold claims to the veracity of their eyewitness accounts if they were self-consciously writing legend or fiction.

Although we do not have the original documents themselves, we have more manuscript evidence of copies of the original documents than we do of any other ancient book or document known to us today. For example, we have a fragment of a New Testament manuscript dating only 50 years after the original document was written (recently fragments were found possibly from the Book of Mark dating to only 25 years after the original was written, but scholars are still verifying those fragments); we have manuscripts of two complete books dating 100 years after the original was written; we have complete manuscripts of most of the New Testament dating to only 150 years after the originals; and we have complete manuscripts of the entire New Testament that date only 225 years after the originals. Moreover, we have over 5,600 copies of these different complete Greek manuscripts copied only 225 years after the originals, and when we compare them we find that we can construct the original documents to a 99 percent degree of accuracy.

Compare this manuscript record with the manuscript evidence for Homer's *Iliad*: we have only around 640 copies and the earliest copy dates to over 500 years after the original, yet we trust that we have a reliable copy. Consider the writings of Plato: we have only seven manuscript copies and the earliest dates to over 1,200 years after the original, yet we trust in the relative authenticity of the copy we now have. Similarly, the *History* of Herodotus: we have only eight copies, dating to 1,350 years after the original, yet we are confident in determining that we have a reliable version of his book. Given that we have over 5,600 copies of Greek New Testament fragments and manuscripts, from as early as 25 years after the originals to only 225 years after the original, it is reasonable to conclude that we have an authentic and reliable version of the original New Testament documents. Finally, it is important to note that even if we did not have any surviving manuscripts, we could easily reconstruct the entire New Testament (all but eleven verses) just from the writings of the early church fathers of the first and second centuries, who quoted extensively from the New Testament documents. This is further evidence that the New Testament that we have today is uncorrupted and unchanged and is thus a reliable copy of the original.

Another reasonable question is: can we trust what these New Testament writers were saying? (I'm trying to preempt some of your possible follow-up questions.) We have an accurate copy of their writings, but did they write the truth or did they fabricate religious stories? As noted above, writers such as Luke, Paul, John, and Peter challenged their contemporary readers to verify their historical accounts, and they provided specific evidence that could be easily verified by their readers. Writers of myth and fantasy do not encourage their readers to verify the veracity of their narratives. Luke, who wrote the Gospel of Luke and the book of Acts (a history of the early church from the resurrection of Christ to just before the destruction of Jerusalem in 70 AD), starts both books referring to the evidence he has compiled so as to encourage his main reader (Theophilus), as well as others who read these books, to believe in the historical reliability of his narratives.

Luke was a trained physician and quite adept at recording his observations and compiling the testimony of others. As it turns out, he was also a remarkably careful and precise historian. In the Gospel of Luke and the book of Acts there are more than one hundred verified historical facts, details, events, places, and names that prove Luke was an eyewitness to what he recorded and that the other eyewitness information he includes is accurate and reliable. Since Matthew and Mark both report the same basic narratives as does Luke, then the reliability of their Gospels is also well established. Moreover, Matthew was a tax collector and, like today, many people in the first century tried to cheat on their taxes. First-century tax collectors were generally suspicious people and quite good at spotting a scam. The fact that Matthew believed so sincerely in the truth and reality of what he saw and then decided to write one of the New Testament Gospels speaks to the reliability of what he recorded. Finally, historians have also verified more than sixty historical details in the Gospel of John, thus testifying to the reliability of this book as well.

Without question, these writers of the New Testament were recording eyewitness accounts and providing historically accurate information. If they were careful in recording these verified historical details, then we have no compelling reason to doubt that they were equally careful and accurate in their recording of other details not (yet) verified. To conclude otherwise is to violate a basic principle in historical scholarship: when a document is proven reliable in recording major historical events, then we must trust that the rest is equally reliable and accurate until proven otherwise. Such historical documents are innocent until proven guilty, so to speak. This operating methodology is afforded to all historical documents, and if we are to be academically consistent and intellectually honest, then this principle should be granted to the New Testament documents as well. Scholarly evidence strongly supports the claim that the New Testament documents are historically accurate and reliable. If the New Testament writers "got it right" on the various historical and archeological details of their first-century lives, then it makes sense to conclude that they also "got it right" in recording the historical events of Christ, including his teachings, trial, crucifixion, burial, and resurrection.

Interestingly, the historical narrative presented by the New Testament historical documents is consistent with the historical record presented by at least ten other non-Christian first- and second-century historical documents. In other words, the New Testament record is corroborated by other nonbiblical historical accounts that were not associated with the writers and writings of the New Testament documents. If we compile historical evidence from such first- and second-century historical writers as Josephus, Tacitus, Pliny the Younger, Phlegon, Thallus, Suetonius, Lucian, Mara Bar-Serapion, and the Jewish Talmud, the following narrative can be constructed: Jesus lived during the time of Tiberius Caesar; he was a virtuous man and lived a virtuous life; he was a wonder-worker; one of his brothers was named James; many claimed he was the Messiah; he was crucified under the governorship of Pontius Pilate; he was crucified on the eve of the Jewish Passover; darkness and an earthquake occurred when he died; Jesus was buried in a tomb; later the tomb was found empty; his disciples and other followers believed he rose from the dead; his disciples and followers were willing to die for their belief; this new religion (Christianity) spread from Jerusalem throughout the Roman empire, as far as Rome itself; his disciples and followers denied the Roman gods and worshiped Jesus as God.

Remember that this historical narrative is constructed from non-Christian writers writing nonbiblical texts, and some of these sources can be considered anti-Christian sources or hostile witnesses, to borrow a legal term. These sources have no stake in supporting the New Testament record. Yet, the basic narrative of the New Testament documents is clearly corroborated by these non-Christian historical documents, and the fact that some of these sources are hostile witnesses lends greater legitimacy to the New Testament record. Of course, it doesn't necessarily mean that all the claims made by the New Testament writers about the meaning and significance of the events are necessarily true, but it does mean that these authors were writing history, and this history is confirmed by other first-century historical writers. Finally, if the New Testament writers are truthful about what they saw happening, then why assume they are not truthful about their explanations of or convictions about what it all meant?

I am quite convinced that the New Testament is not myth, folklore, or legend; rather, it is history, and reliable history at that. But, as I've said in some of my other messages, don't take my word for it. Below are several resources that explore these issues in much more detail. I hope you will research them for yourself.

Barnett, Paul. *Is the New Testament Reliable?* Downers Grove, IL: InterVarsity, 1986.

———. *Jesus and the Logic of History.* Grand Rapids: Eerdmans, 1997.

Blomberg, Craig. *The Historical Reliability of the Gospels.* Downers Grove, IL: InterVarsity, 1987.

Bruce, F. F. *The Canon of Scripture.* Downers Grove, IL: InterVarsity, 1988.

———. *Jesus and Christian Origins outside the New Testament.* Grand Rapids: Eerdmans, 1974.

———. *The New Testament Documents: Are They Reliable?* Grand Rapids: Eerdmans, 2003.

Craig, William Lane. *Reasonable Faith: Christian Truth and Apologetics.* Wheaton, IL: Crossway, 1994.

France, R. T. *The Evidence for Jesus.* Downers Grove, IL: InterVarsity, 1986.

Geisler, Norman. *Christian Apologetics.* Grand Rapids: Baker, 1976.

Geisler, Norman, and Frank Turek. *I Don't Have Enough Faith to Be an Atheist.* Wheaton, IL: Crossway, 2004.

Geisler, Norman L., and William E. Nix. *A General Introduction to the Bible.* Chicago: Moody, 1986.

Habermas, Gary. *The Historical Jesus: Ancient Evidence for the Life of Christ.* Joplin, MO: College, 1996.

Kenyon, Fredric. *Our Bible and the Ancient Manuscripts.* New York: Harper & Row, 1958.

Kreeft, Peter. *Making Sense Out of Suffering.* Ann Arbor: Servant Books, 1986.

Lewis, C. S. *Christian Reflections*. Ed. Walter Hoop. Grand Rapids: Eerdmans, 1967.

McDowell, Josh. *The New Evidence that Demands a Verdict*. Nashville: Thomas Nelson, 1999.

Wow, I think this message is longer than the previous, so let me bring it to a close. I hope this helps a bit. I have a feeling, though, that you will have some more questions.

Cheers,
Prof. Dave

Exchange 10

Isn't It Irrational to Believe in Miracles These Days?

Dear Prof,

Whoa . . . did you burn up your keyboard on that last message? You gave me a lot of information I had never heard before, and thanks for the reading list. I think you are providing me more readings than my regular college courses. Ha ha. Many of your points make sense, and I have some more thinking to do. To be honest, though, I'm not so sure I can accept the New Testament as history. After all, don't its books mention miracles and other supernatural occurrences? It's my understanding that history doesn't contain stories of the miraculous. Don't we automatically call such narratives myths or fantasies? I know you said that the style of writing in the New Testament is not typically mythological, but doesn't the presence of the fantastic or the supernatural make the New Testament by definition mythology?

Sincerely,
Seeker

Dear Seeker,

You sure are pulling out the big guns here! I thought my last response would give you enough to chew on for a while, but you are asking the logical next question. The short answer to your question is simply—no: the presence of the miraculous in a narrative does not make it ipso facto mythology. I know this short answer will not satisfy you (nor should it), and it doesn't adequately acknowledge the sincerity of your question. So, let me explain more fully.

The question, I think, is basically this: because the New Testament contains miracles and resurrections (that's right, the New Testament records more than one resurrection), then surely it cannot be history, can it? Well, my response is, why not? Again, if the writers were careful in how they recorded other historically reliable facts, events, names, and places, then what is the justification for concluding that they would be any less careful or truthful about recording what is wondrous, like miracles and resurrections? Notice that even the non-Christian first- and second-century historians record that Jesus was a wonder-worker. They didn't try to rationalize the deeds or explain them away; they merely reported that he performed wondrous acts. Even Jewish Talmudic writings claim Jesus performed miracles, and they often characterize Jesus as a sorcerer. It's important to note that these other first- and second-century historical writings do not try to deny or explain the miraculous away—they simply report what was observed. Are we supposed to dismiss these non-Christian historians as well because they also state that Jesus performed wondrous acts?

It is true, however, that the New Testament provides more specific details surrounding the miracles, but that is because these New Testament documents were written by eyewitnesses and contemporaries of the eyewitnesses. Remember that any false claims in the New Testament record could have easily been refuted by the contemporaries. We have no evidence of other eyewitnesses trying to refute the claims of the New Testament writers. Also note that the style of the first-century New Testament writers is one of historical documentation: facts are given in an unembellished way. Fable, myth, and lore do not have historically verifiable information, and these story forms are told with great literary embellishment. We simply do not see this in the New Testament historical narratives. However, we do see such ahistorical embellishment in the later second- and third-century gnostic gospels, which are distortions of historical fact. It is curious that some scholars today are willing to accept the ahistorical writings of the gnostics, which were written centuries after the fact by people who were not eyewitnesses to the original events, yet these scholars are unwilling to accept the historical record of the New Testament writers who were eyewitnesses or contemporaries of eyewitnesses to the actual events.

Other thoughtful critics may claim that we must reject the New Testament as history simply because it presents miracles as true, factual occurrences. However, to what extent is this argument close-minded and ultimately self-defeating? We can all agree that academic integrity and honesty require that we be as open-minded as possible when considering the facts. We can also agree that we should avoid presupposing our conclusions; that is, we should not rule out certain conclusions from the very beginning without fully considering the data. Rejecting the historicity of the New Testament simply because there are narrative accounts of miracles is a close-minded conclusion based upon an unsupported presupposition that there is no such thing as a miracle. This is the uncritical bias of naturalism: some people will only accept natural explanations for all perceived phenomena. However, such a perspective stacks the deck in its favor, so to speak, and it simply dismisses out of hand anything that contains evidence or records of the miraculous, because it has decided ahead of time not to believe in the possibility of the miraculous. Such a view basically amounts to believing what you want to believe regardless of the evidence to the contrary. That is the epitome of arrogant close-mindedness. This naturalistic view offers no proof or explanation for its conclusion; it merely asserts the naturalistic presupposition as true. So, it has arrived at its conclusion before the analysis even begins. Such circular logical reasoning is most problematic.

But wait a minute; aren't most naturalists basing their presupposition upon the conclusion of David Hume, whose views on empiricism soundly refuted the possibility of miracles? Let's test that position. C. S. Lewis in his book *Miracles* (1960), Norman L. Geisler in his book *Miracles and the Modern Mind* (1992), and Ronald H. Nash in his book *Faith and Reason* (1994) all carefully argue that Hume clearly denied the miraculous, but he did not logically refute or empirically disprove it. Here is Hume's basic line of reasoning on the matter of miracles: (1) natural law is a description of a regular occurrence; (2) a miracle is a rare occurrence; (3) the evidence for the regular is always greater than the evidence for the rare; (4) a wise man bases his belief on the greater evidence; (5) therefore, a wise man should never believe in miracles. Well, there you have it. Sounds reasonable enough. Except for one thing: premise three is not necessarily true. That is, evidence for the regular is not always greater than evidence for the rare.

We need only one counter-example to disprove this premise, but let's consider several counter-examples. Here are a few historical occurrences that are believed by most naturalists and empiricists to be true despite the fact each of them are rare events: (1) the origin of the universe happened only once (indeed, some naturalists do not believe that the universe had a beginning, but the wealth of current scientific data argues otherwise);

(2) the origin of life happened only once (most naturalists believe life came from nonlife spontaneously and this event happened only once with no one there to observe it); (3) the origin of new life happens only once (again, most naturalists believe in macroevolutionary processes that bring new life into existence and this happens only once, unobserved, for each new life form); and (4) the entire history of the world is comprised of rare, unrepeatable events (even Hume's own birth is a singular, rare, and unrepeatable event). Naturalists believe that each of these events actually occurred, yet if they really followed Hume's logic, they would have to reject them as false, just as they reject miracles for being false, because they are rare, unrepeatable events. In this sense, Hume's argument against miracles is self-defeating, if not completely irrational, because its logic forces rational people to deny their own experiences of rare events that they know to be rationally true (for example, they would have to deny their own birth and other such rare events).

Moreover, as Lewis, Geisler, and Nash argue, Hume's anti-miracles view confuses believability with possibility: it indeed may challenge the *believability* of miracles, but it does not refute the *possibility* of the miraculous. In other words, it may be difficult to believe in miracles, but given the existence of God (as established in our earlier exchanges), it is indeed possible for miracles to occur. Also, Hume's view confuses probability with evidence. It doesn't weigh the evidence for the individual rare event; rather, it dismisses belief in the rare based upon the unlikely probability of it occurring or not. But, there are many rare events that we believe because of the weight of the evidence of that singular, rare event: one's own birth, being accepted to the top college of your choice, or winning the lottery, for example. Each of these is a rare, unrepeatable event, yet there is much evidence for each singular event. Plus, there is much indirect evidence for such events, observable by many people after the fact: that you are now alive attests to your being born, that you are in college attests your being accepted into college, that you are receiving regular checks from the lottery commission proves that you won the lottery. Finally, Hume correctly defines a miracle as a rare event, but then he punishes it for being a rare event. (That hardly seems fair.) He says we shouldn't believe in miracles because they are rare and unrepeatable; if they were repeatable we could believe them. But, ironically, if they were repeatable (and thus no longer rare) then according to his own definition they would no longer be miracles. You see the problem? According to his view we could only believe in miracles if they were by definition not miracles. Such a view does not disprove miracles; it merely makes impossible that which it is trying to disprove to begin with. This is circular reasoning—it starts with its conclusion and then argues toward that same conclusion. It assumes from the beginning that miracles cannot exist and then proceeds to prove they cannot exist. In the end, such an argument does not really disprove miracles at all.

Disbelief in miracles is more a matter of the will than one of intellect or logic. Some would rather not believe in the miraculous because they do not like the implications of conceding the possibility of miracles. The larger point here is that it is not logically warranted or intellectually honest to discount miracles from the very beginning of an inquiry into the possibility of the miraculous—simply arriving at your conclusion before the analysis even begins. That is not very open-minded, intellectually honest, or even logical. If we are to examine this question of the historicity or mythology of the New Testament, the miracles, and the resurrection honestly and fairly (which the question itself deserves), then we should strive to be as open-minded, fair, and reasonable as possible. Dismissing the occurrence of miracles out of hand, based upon presuppositional bias, problematic reasoning, and circular argumentation, does not qualify as honest, fair, and open inquiry.

So, all that is to say: no, the presence of the miraculous in the New Testament record does not automatically dismiss it as nonhistorical and does not thus relegate it to the genre of myth or fantasy. Naturalists and empiricists will say that it is irrational to believe in miracles, but I hope my discussion here has demonstrated that their rationale for not believing in the possibility of the miraculous is itself an irrational faith. I've really only scratched the surface of this issue and tried to give you a structured overview. If you want to investigate the intricacies of the arguments on both sides, consider (yet again) some more reading:

> Geisler, Norman L. *Miracles and the Modern Mind.* Grand Rapids: Baker, 1992.
>
> Geisler, Norman L., and Ronald M. Brooks. *When Skeptics Ask.* Wheaton, IL: Victor, 1990.
>
> Geivett, Douglas, and Gary R. Habermas. *Defense of Miracles.* Downers Grove, IL: InterVarsity Press, 1997.
>
> Kreeft, Peter. *Christianity for Modern Pagans.* San Francisco: Ignatius Press, 1993.

Kreeft, Peter, and Ronald Tacelli. *Handbook of Christian Apologetics.* Downers Grove, IL: InterVarsity Press, 1994.

Lewis, C. S. *Miracles.* New York: Macmillan, 1960.

Nash, Ronald H. *Reason and Faith.* Grand Rapids: Zondervan, 1994.

Your question is meaningful and quite serious, and I hope you find my response serious and meaningful as well. Please review these ideas, do some follow-up reading, and let me know if you have other questions. As always, keep thinking, keep asking questions, but also sincerely consider the answers and information provided. It's somewhat easy to ask questions, but it is far more challenging to engage the answers. It is my prayer that these exchanges are helping you on your journey toward finding answers and truth.

Cheers,
Prof. Dave

Exchange 11

But, the Resurrection of Christ Is Just a Myth, Right?

Dear Prof,

Sorry I haven't written for a while. I've been really busy with my schoolwork, but also I've been thinking a lot about your last message. It reminded me of some philosophy courses I've taken. I remember Hume and empiricism, but I certainly don't remember the professor discussing the self-defeating logic of Hume's argument against miracles. That was a bit of a mind bender, and I'm going to have to review your message and some of the sources you mentioned. But even if we agree that some miracles are possible (and even probable), do we really have any good reason to believe in the resurrection of Jesus Christ? I mean, come on, isn't it just too much to accept that a dead person came back to life? That has to be a myth, doesn't it?

Sincerely,
Seeker

Dear Seeker,

It's really good to hear from you. I was wondering what was going on and figured you were probably swamped with reading, tests, and papers. I'm so glad you are continuing to think through the philosophical and logical elements of Hume's skepticism regarding the miraculous. Keep at it.

I must admit that the resurrection of Christ is an incredible historical claim. Yet, all scholars agree, whether they are skeptical about the resurrection or not, that the New Testament documents clearly attest to the historical facts of the crucifixion of Jesus, his death, his burial, the discovery of his empty tomb, and the resurrection. Many readers can conclude that since the New Testament writers are accurate, honest, and trustworthy on the natural historical occurrences, then they can be trusted on the supernatural historical occurrences. Others say, not so fast.

Some skeptics argue that the New Testament writers indeed are writing history, but they simply got it wrong when it comes to the resurrection. On all other matters they were right, but on this one matter they were deceived. Clearly, they sincerely believed that they saw the risen Jesus, but maybe they were simply mistaken. After all, you can be sincere and still be wrong. Many skeptics suggest that maybe there are some naturalistic explanations for the resurrection. Fair enough, so let's critically examine some of the major alternative explanations for the empty tomb and the reported sightings of the resurrected Jesus, and let's see if they adequately refute the possibility of the resurrection or, in the very least, if they provide a more reasonable explanation for the empty tomb.

HALLUCINATION THEORY

Some critics suggest that maybe the disciples were hallucinating when they saw the resurrected Jesus and simply recorded what they thought to be true. The problem with this explanation is that hallucinations result from very rare and specific psychological conditions, and there is no evidence to suggest that all of these witnesses and writers suffered from hallucinations. Moreover, hallucinations happen to individuals in singular moments. Your own hallucination cannot also occur simultaneously to your friends, family, and hundreds of other people. (Paul records in his first letter to the Corinthians that the resurrected Jesus appeared to Cephas, to the other apostles, to James the brother of Jesus, to more than five hundred other people, and then to himself. See 1 Cor 15:5–7.) Also, Jesus' appearances occurred over a forty-day period of time, and most of them were corporeal appearances in which different witnesses (at different times) touched Jesus or ate with him. Hallucinations are not physical and are not sustained over long periods of time.

We should also note that hallucinations involve images or visions of what the person may expect to see or witness in real life. In other words, people generally do not hallucinate what they do not already expect to be true or real or possible. In the first century, many Jews did not believe in resurrection at all (so they would not have hallucinated that which they did not believe possible), and others (including the disciples and most of their followers) who did believe in bodily resurrection believed that it would happen all at once for all people at the end of time. Since the disciples did not have this general expectation of bodily resurrection before the end of time, it is not likely that they would have envisioned in a hallucination this kind of resurrection for Jesus. Moreover, they did not expect their Messiah to be killed, let alone be individually resurrected; thus it is most improbable for them to hallucinate the resurrection of their slain Messiah. Finally, this hallucination theory does not address the empty tomb (a well-established historical fact). If they were simply hallucinating the risen Jesus, then why was the tomb empty? Their hallucinations would have been immediately dispelled by the real body in the tomb.

WITNESSES WENT TO THE WRONG TOMB

It has been suggested that the women who first discovered the empty tomb and then the disciples simply went to the wrong tomb, found it empty, and mistakenly proclaimed Jesus had risen. The obvious problem here is that the Jewish and Roman authorities would have quickly pointed out this error and would have directed them to the correct tomb wherein they would have found the dead Jesus. Also, this theory does not explain the various appearances of the risen Jesus (both the empty tomb and the appearances must be explained). Note that in the New Testament historical record, most of the disciples were not convinced that Jesus had risen just from finding the tomb empty; rather, once they saw, touched, and spent time with the resurrected Jesus, they finally became convinced of the truth of his various teachings and messianic claims. This wrong tomb theory simply does not explain the empty tomb, the appearances of the risen Jesus, or why the disciples were ultimately convinced Jesus had risen from the grave.

Another interesting note: the fact that the New Testament writers report that women were the first to find the tomb empty and reported back to the cowering men that Jesus had risen further attests to the authenticity and reliability of the report. In Near Eastern cultures of the first century, the testimony of women was not considered valid. It was rather embarrassing for these male disciples that the women were the ones bold enough to leave their homes and visit the tomb. The men feared persecution and were hiding. Moreover, the testimony of women was not highly valued in this culture. Yet, in the reports of these events, the New Testament writers include the part about the women's testimony. If they were making this all up and wanted others to believe their fabricated story, then they would not have included the testimony of women, which in their culture would not have been considered valid or credible. Moreover, the writers would have represented themselves in a more flattering light if they were making it all up. The narratives of the women going to the tomb and finding it empty are included simply because it actually happened that way. The wrong tomb theory fails to address these crucial historical and cultural realities.

SWOON OR APPARENT DEATH THEORY

Is it possible that Jesus merely fainted or swooned on the cross, that people only assumed he was dead, and that he later recovered in the tomb? Or, could it be that Jesus took a narcotic drug that gave him the appearance of death, and he later revived in the tomb? These are interesting hypothetical questions. But, remember, both friends and enemies of Jesus believed he was dead. The Romans were experts at execution by crucifixion, and they knew if someone was dead or not. Historical records show that Jesus was severely beaten to the point of collapse, he dragged his own cross to the point of exhaustion, large spikes were hammered into his wrists and feet, and a spear was plunged into his side, puncturing his heart and releasing blood and water, confirming, according to modern medical experts, that he was in fact dead. We should also note that the Roman guards did not have to break his legs to bring on death by asphyxiation, because they knew him to be already dead. Pilate confirmed for himself that Jesus was dead, and all the disciples were in despair because they knew him to be truly dead. Joseph of Arimathea and Nicodemus embalmed the dead Jesus in seventy-five pounds of spices and bandages; they would not have mistakenly embalmed a live man. Even if he were alive, he would have bled to death in the tomb and/or suffocated from the embalming and wrapping procedure.

It is also unreasonable to think that a horribly beaten and crucified person—even if he did survive this execution technique—could have unwrapped himself, rolled way the two-ton stone covering the tomb, slipped past the elite Roman guards, and then convinced a fearful group of disciples that he in his bloody, battered, bruised, and weak condition had triumphed over death. Furthermore, this theory does not explain the supernatural appearance of Jesus to Paul on the road to Damascus, an experience that radically transformed this feared persecutor of early Christian believers into the most influential advocate for the veracity of the Christian message. Certainly, a normal human being who had apparently recovered from a near-death crucifixion experience could not have effected such a change in the exceptionally brilliant and well-educated Paul. Also, non-Christian first-century writers, such as Josephus, Tacitus, and Thallus, who were unsympathetic to the followers of Jesus, also wrote that he had indeed died by crucifixion. Finally, the Jewish Talmud confirms that Jesus was crucified on the eve of the Passover. Very few scholars actually believe the swoon theory, because there is simply too much evidence against it, not to mention no evidence for it (it is merely hypothetical).

THE DISCIPLES STOLE THE BODY

Some skeptics suggest that the disciples stole and hid the body and then made up the whole resurrection story to justify a new religion. The problem with this theory is that it does not support the skeptics' claim that the disciples were themselves deceived and simply reported what they thought to be true. This theory claims that the disciples were the deceivers. This view is further unreasonable because it cannot explain why these disciples would subject themselves to ridicule, excommunication from the temple, persecution, torture, and even execution, all for a lie of their own making. At the first sign of major trouble, they simply would have confessed to the deception and that would be that.

Also, if they stole the body, how did they get past the elite Roman guards? If Jesus never really rose from the dead, then who appeared to Paul and James and more than five hundred other eyewitnesses? Did the New Testament writers lie about the conversions of Paul and James and many others? What about all the letters that we know Paul wrote—are they all somehow lies? Why would Paul, who was persecuting and executing Christians, suddenly change his mind and be the greatest advocate for his former enemies? What about the claims of non-Christian writers? Did Josephus lie about James being martyred by the Sanhedrin for his belief in the risen Jesus? Did the Roman writer Phlegon lie when he wrote about the resurrected Jesus in his historical book *Chronicles*? This theory is what the Jewish authorities offered at the time as an explanation for the empty tomb. However, it fails for the above mentioned reasons. Moreover, we know it to be false because the Jewish authorities had to pay off the Roman guards to buy their silence and then promise to keep them out of trouble with the governor. You do not have to bribe or pay off honest witnesses to the truth.

SOMEONE ELSE TOOK JESUS' PLACE ON THE CROSS

Some people believe that someone else, like Judas, was executed on the cross in the place of Jesus. In fact, this is what the Qur'an states in Sura 4:157–58. However, the Qur'anic account was written roughly six hundred years later, and it is not reasonable to believe it over the eyewitness accounts of those who actually saw what happened. Some point to the Gospel of Barnabas as evidence in support of this theory. Yet, most scholars agree that this gospel is a forgery, probably written in the fifteenth century. Additionally, this theory contradicts the non-Christian historical sources from the first-century that attest to the execution of Jesus. It seems a bit far-fetched to believe that the disciples, Jesus' family and friends, the Roman guards, Pilate, and the Jewish authorities were all mistaken about what they saw and confirmed to be true.

There are other issues to consider with this theory as well. If Jesus really didn't die on the cross but someone else did, then what happened to that substitute's body? Why was his tomb empty? Did he rise from the dead? Or, was his body somehow stolen out from under the noses of the elite Roman guards and hidden? According to the Qur'anic account, Jesus was taken up to Allah directly, so who was it that appeared to so many people? Who changed Paul's mind? The resurrected substitute? To believe the substitute theory requires that we believe all the evidence to the contrary is wrong and that all the New Testament writers, the non-Christian first-century writers, Pilate, the Roman guards, and the Jewish authorities were all wrong or somehow deceived. This theory is based upon speculation with no evidence to support it.

THE DISCIPLE'S FAITH LED TO THEIR BELIEF IN THE RESURRECTION

John Dominic Crossan and others of "The Jesus Seminar" claim that the disciples made up the resurrection story after Jesus' death to support their faith. In short, this theory claims that their faith led to their belief in the resurrection. The problem with this theory is that there is no evidence to support it, and it actually gets the history backwards. The accounts from the New Testament writers and from the non-Christian first-century historians all affirm that the disciples had no faith after Jesus was crucified, but then suddenly after having seen him resurrected they had a faith so strong that they were willing to be tortured and murdered for their belief instead of renouncing it as a lie. Their faith did not lead to the resurrection story; rather, the resurrection event led to their faith. Also, this theory does not explain the recorded appearance of Jesus to over five hundred people, nor does it explain the empty tomb and the fact that the Jewish authorities continued to insist through the second century that the disciples stole the body. This alternative theory is the most problematic of them all and has not a shred of evidence to support it. If you are looking for fantasy or myth, this theory is a good one.

THE NEW TESTAMENT WRITERS BORROWED FROM PAGAN RESURRECTION MYTHS

This is probably the most frequently cited counter-theory to explain the resurrection. Skeptics claim that the New Testament documents are not historical and that they are simply copying from pagan mythology, citing as examples the resurrection myths of such characters as Marduk, Adonis, and Osiris. As we have already seen, the New Testament is not written in the style of mythology, it does not have fantastical embellishments (unlike some of the gnostic gospels written centuries later), and it contains hundreds of confirmed historical facts about first-century life, events, people, and geography. Myths do not contain such a preponderance of historical elements. The pagan myth theory does not explain the empty tomb, the martyrdom of eyewitnesses, or the historical testimony of the non-Christian writers. Why would the non-Christian historians of the first and second centuries confirm a Christian myth? Also, the first-century Jewish and pagan critics of the new Christian religion knew that the New Testament writers were making historical claims, not mythical ones, and they disputed the plausibility of the claims, not the reality or historicity of them.

Furthermore, there are no Greek or Roman myths that speak of a literal incarnation of a monotheistic God into a human body by way of a virgin birth that was followed by a literal death and bodily resurrection. The Greeks and Romans were polytheists, not monotheists like the New Testament writers, and the Greeks believed in reincarnation into a different mortal body, while the New Testament writers wrote about a resurrection of the same physical body that was transformed or translated into an immortal form. The first real parallel in pagan myth of a dying and rising god does not appear until AD 150 (more than 100 years after the start of Christianity), so if anything it was the Christian religion that influenced this emerging pagan myth. The Egyptian cult of Osiris does predate Christianity and it does have a mythical account of a god surviving death, but it is nothing like what the New Testament writers describe. In this myth, Osiris dies and is cut into fourteen pieces and spread all over Egypt. Then, the goddess Isis pieces him back together and brings him back to life, but he exists only in some shadowy form in the underworld. This myth is nothing like the New Testament writers' description of a triumphantly glorified resurrected Jesus who appears to many people in physical form for an extended period of time and then ascends into Heaven. Finally, even if there were similar pagan myths, we cannot conclude derivation from similarity (that is, just because two things are similar does not then mean that one derived from the other). There simply is no compelling evidence to support the claim that the New Testament writers wrote mythology and borrowed their material from pagan resurrection myths.

It is relatively easy to come up with variant narratives and other hypothetical possibilities, but we must ask the basic question: is there evidence to support the alternative theory and does that theory best explain all the historical events, namely the empty tomb, the Jewish attempts to explain the empty tomb, the boldness of the disciples to proclaim their new faith in a risen Jesus even under persecution and the threat of death, the abandonment of an ancient religion and the birth of a new religion based upon historical events, and the spread of this new religion in the face of cruel persecution, torture, and execution? I think it reasonable to be skeptical about the skeptics' alternatives. Using the principle of arguing from the best explanation (a strategy used by science, by the way), we can make the following reasonable claim: Given the facts and the various possible theories, the best theory that has the most evidence, that makes the most sense of all the historical facts, and that has the greatest explanatory power is the very claim that the New Testament writers wrote about and for which many of them died—that Jesus in fact rose from the dead.

The resurrection is also strong historical evidence substantiating Jesus' claim to be God in the flesh. If God exists, and we have examined many good reasons to believe he does, then miracles are indeed possible. What greater miracle can there be, and thus clear proof of the existence of God, than the miracle of overcoming death? Only God can create out of nothing and thus bring life out of death. That Jesus defeated death and rose from the dead is strong evidence for his claim to be God. Some critics assert that Jesus never claimed to be God, but the reliable New Testament record has many examples of Jesus clearly asserting his identity as God. For example, in Mark 14:61–64 Jesus is asked by the high priest Caiaphas if he is the Christ, the Son of God, and Jesus replies directly, "I am, and you will see the Son of Man seated at the right hand of Power, and coming with the clouds of heaven" (v. 62). Caiaphas and the others are shocked and outraged, because they clearly understand Jesus' claim to be God, and they condemn him for blasphemy, for claiming to be God. This direct claim is recorded also in Matthew chapter 27 and Luke chapter 22.

Jesus makes a more explicit claim to deity in John chapter 8. During a heated discussion with a group of people, Jesus makes a curious and seemingly ungrammatical statement: "Truly, truly, I say to you, before Abraham was, I am" (John 8:58). Here, Jesus says that he is the eternal God, the Great I AM who preexisted Abraham (the ancient father of the Jews). He uses the same name for God (I AM) that God used when he revealed himself to Moses, referring to himself as I AM (that is, the necessary being, the eternally existing entity that has always been in existence and who has brought all created things into existence). The crowd immediately understands what Jesus clearly means—that he is God—and they pick up stones and try to stone him for blasphemy. Jesus also made many other implicit claims to deity: he claimed glory that is only rightfully God's, he accepted worship from man that only God deserves, he forgave sins as only God can, and his disciples taught throughout the New Testament that Jesus is God.[1] The larger point here is that since the New Testament record is reliable, and since it testifies to Jesus' many claims to deity and offers evidence of the resurrection, then it is indeed reasonable to believe that Jesus is who he claimed to be—the living God.

Well, it seems I've written quite a bit, once again. I know this is a lot to take in, but you are asking very important questions, and I'm trying to treat your inquiries with the proper respect and diligence they deserve. I firmly believe there is compelling evidence to have a reasonable and logical faith in the resurrection of Jesus. There are plenty of other highly intelligent people who believe in the resurrection. The following is a list of such people and their intellectual work on this subject. I encourage you to review their research and conclusions:

---

1. For an excellent outline and discussion of these and other examples of Jesus claiming to be God, see Geisler and Turek, *I Don't Have Enough Faith to Be an Atheist*, 340–48.

Boyd, Gregory A. *Cynic, Sage, or Son of God?* Grand Rapids: Baker, 1995.

Craig, William Lane. *Reasonable Faith: Christian Truth and Apologetics.* Wheaton, IL: Crossway, 1994.

———. *The Son Rises: The Historical Evidence for the Resurrection of Jesus.* Eugene, OR: Wipf & Stock, 2001.

Geisler, Norman. *Christian Apologetics.* Grand Rapids: Baker, 1976.

Geisler, Norman, and Frank Turek. *I Don't Have Enough Faith to Be an Atheist.* Wheaton, IL: Crossway, 2004.

Habermas, Gary. *The Case for the Resurrection of Jesus.* Grand Rapids: Kregel, 2004.

———. *The Historical Jesus: Ancient Evidence for the Life of Christ.* Joplin, MO: College Press, 1996.

Lewis, C. S. *Mere Christianity.* 1952. New York: HarperCollins, 2001.

McDowell, Josh. *The New Evidence that Demands a Verdict.* Nashville: Thomas Nelson, 1999.

Moreland, J. P. *Scaling the Secular City: A Defense of Christianity.* Grand Rapids: Baker, 1987.

Stott, John R. W. *The Cross of Christ.* Downers Grove, IL: InterVarsity, 1986.

Cheers,
Prof. Dave

Exchange 12

The Reliability of the New Testament Makes Sense To Me, but Why Should We Trust the Reliability of the Old Testament? That Just Seems Too Far-Fetched

Dear Prof,

Thank you so much for all the information you provided on the resurrection of Christ. Over the years, I've heard some of the alternative explanations for the resurrection that you mentioned, but I haven't heard them analyzed or refuted. I've spent the last month or so mulling it over, and I even read through some of the resources you mentioned. I have more studying and thinking to do, but for the most part, it makes a lot of sense. I may not fully agree just yet, but I understand how and why the New Testament can (and even should) be considered a reliable historical account of Jesus' life and teachings and a trustworthy record of the teachings of the disciples that laid the foundation for true Christianity. This is very reasonable to me. However, here recently I've been reading parts of the Old Testament, and I'm having a difficult time. A lot of it just seems wacked! Are we to trust the Old Testament as reliable, true history like the New Testament? That just seems a bit far-fetched.

Sincerely,
Seeker

Dear Seeker,

I'm so glad you are continuing to think through these issues, and I'm happy that the reading list I sent was helpful to you. It's obvious to me that you are really engaging this material, because you have asked yet another really important question regarding the nature and reliability of the Old Testament writings. I hope I can do your question justice.

It is important to note that many Christians also have a lot of questions about the Old Testament, and there are a variety of views within the Christian community. Let me share with you my own point of view on this issue, and I hope you find it helpful. As I studied and reflected upon the Old Testament, I came to the realization that how I viewed the Old Testament depended ultimately upon what I understood about the person and nature of Jesus Christ. Some people will say that he was just a great moral teacher. But, if you think about it, this view just doesn't go far enough. Jesus quite clearly claimed (and proved, as we discussed in our last exchange) to be God. (Note that many men have claimed to be God, but there is only one God who took on human form and walked among humans within history—that is Jesus Christ, who is unique in all ways. If you have doubts about this, reread the Gospel of John.) If Christ is not God, then he was a liar or a lunatic. C. S. Lewis does a great job in his book *Mere Christianity* of explaining that these are your basic choices about the identity of Jesus: he is liar, lunatic, or Lord.[1] The reliable New Testament record does not leave much room for any other option.

Notice that if Christ is ultimately not the Lord God, then he is either a liar or a lunatic. He directly claimed to be God, and if he is not, then he was purposefully lying or he was a crazy man, and neither of these categories fit what we generally understand as being a truly great moral teacher (a liar cannot be a morally good person, and an insane man cannot possess the proper faculty of mind to be a good teacher). So, it is not logically satisfying, given all the evidence, to just conclude Christ was a great moral teacher, but not God. As we've determined, the New Testament historical record and other first-century writers (Jewish, Roman, and Greek) all confirm the following basic historical elements: the life, ministry, and miracles of Christ; his trial, crucifixion, and death; the empty tomb; his appearance to on different occasions to the disciples and then more than five hundred people; the establishment of the early church; the worshiping of Christ as God; the conversion of many Jews from their traditional religion to a

---

1. Lewis, *Mere Christianity*, 52.

relationship with the Living God; and the growth of the church despite harsh persecution. The only logical explanation that is internally consistent and that coherently accounts for all of these historical facts is the resurrection, which confirms his deity. In other words, it is reasonable, given this evidence, to conclude that Jesus is God. We can deny this, but the denial is not a refutation. To reject this evidence and to deny the deity of Jesus is ultimately an act of the will, not a commitment to intellectual inquiry or logical reasoning.

So, the first step for me in coming to trust the reliability of the Old Testament is understanding that Jesus is God. Throughout Christ's life and ministry, he taught from the Old Testament Scriptures. In the New Testament, the terms "Scriptures," "the Law of Moses," "the prophets," and "the Psalms" all refer to the Old Testament writings, the Hebrew Bible. In the teachings of Christ, he anchored his teachings in all the key portions of scripture, from Genesis through to the "minor prophets" (those last several books of the Old Testament that few people have read or even know about). That is, Christ taught from or referenced all of the Old Testament. He didn't view the Old Testament as nice stories or myths, but as God's truth specially revealed to humans through his prophets. Christ, as God who cannot lie and who knows all things clearly, taught from and affirmed the legitimacy, validity, historicity, and veracity of the Old Testament. For the true believer in Christ, that is evidence enough of the reliability and trustworthiness of the Old Testament. Note: this is faith that is based in sound logical thinking, not blind, thoughtless faith. Note, too, that this is the only way to argue that the Old Testament is the true word of God without succumbing to the problem of circular reasoning. Many believers will (understandably) argue that the Old Testament is the word of God because it says so. However, this argument by itself is vulnerable in that it can be attacked for being mere circular logic. The main reason why I trust the Old Testament is because Christ, who is God and who thus knows all things and does not lie, affirmed the reliability, authority, and veracity of the Old Testament. This argument is not circular logic.

Beyond that, we know that the Old Testament is the true word of God because it was declared as such by the Old Testament writers and prophets. Note that this argument, if not carefully formulated or discussed, is also susceptible to the charge of circular logic. However, we can address the circular logic of this argument as follows. The various prophets claimed very sincerely and honestly not to be making things up themselves, but rather were inspired by God. The problem is how to prove this without saying, "Hey, just take my word for it." Just because they were sincere doesn't make them right—they could be sincerely wrong. The major prophets of the Old Testament were often challenged by their audiences (both Hebrews and other Near Easterners who worshiped other gods) to prove that their writings where truly inspired by God. This is where prophecy and miracles come into play. Note that in a theistic universe, prophecy and miracles are indeed possible, and it makes sense that God would use prophecy and miracles to substantiate his message or revelation. (How would we know a message came from a supernatural being such as God? By the presence of the supernatural as a kind of validating stamp.) All of the Old Testament prophets in some way substantiated their writings through accurately fulfilled prophecy or by miraculous deeds that could not be refuted by others. In this way, the Old Testament writings were substantiated as being the inspired word of God. Note that this is a problem for other so-called revealed religions, such as Islam. Mohammed never performed any miracles to substantiate his claim that the Qu'ran is truly from God. He was even challenged to perform miracles in order to prove that he was a prophet, but he could not and did not perform any miracles. There are some legends that were developed well after his life that say he performed miracles, but they are not accepted as true by orthodox Muslims. Mohammed merely said the Qu'ran itself was the miracle. This is circular logic. So, there is no miraculous or prophetic evidentiary support for the Qu'ran. The same is true for the Book of Mormon.

Furthermore, archeology continues to support the Old Testament's historical records. The Old Testament is comprised of many different genres: it is a book of origins, law, prophecy, wisdom, poetry, and history. The various historical books (for example, Kings and Chronicles) are continually being affirmed by archeological studies. There are examples of archeologists during the twentieth century who set out to prove the Old Testament false, only to be convicted by the evidence of its truth and accuracy, and many of these became believers because of it. A book you should get is *The New Evidence that Demands a Verdict* by Josh McDowell, which details these types of archeological evidences in great detail.

Lastly, the recent discovery of the Dead Sea Scrolls has greatly proven the reliability of the Old Testament as we now have it. Before we had the Dead Sea Scrolls, our most ancient copy of the Old Testament dated back to 900 AD. In 1947, the scrolls were discovered and analyzed. They dated to 125 BC, more than a thousand years older than the oldest manuscript we had up to that point. When these scrolls were compared with the later versions of the Old Testament, researchers discovered that the texts were 95 percent accurate! The five percent variance was found to be obvious slips of the transcriber's pen or variations in spelling of words, such that no fundamental change in meaning, text, or context was detected. This is compelling textual evidence to support the reasonable claim that the text of the Old Testament that we have today is the same text that Jesus validated in the first century. In short, we have convincing data to substantiate a reasonable faith in the authority, validity, and reliability of the Old Testament.

So, the Old Testament is verified by Christ (who is God and who would not lie about the authority of his revelation), authenticated by miracles and fulfilled prophecy (that is, marked by the stamp of God—the supernatural), confirmed by archeology, and substantiated by textual consistency. When these lines of reasoning are considered cumulatively, we can see that there is overwhelming evidence for the reliability of the Old Testament. Because of this strong evidence for the Old Testament, along with all the information we already discussed regarding the reliability of the New Testament, I find no good logical reason to disbelieve the validity, veracity, and inspired nature of the whole Bible. Again, you can choose not to believe it, but such a choice is an act of will, not an act of discerning, open-minded reasoning that honestly considers the wealth of evidence available to us today.

As always, don't just take my word for it. Investigate for yourself. As if you didn't have enough to read already, here are some more sources to review (some of which I've mentioned before):

> Albright, William F. *The Archaeology of Palestine*. New York: Penguin, 1949.
>
> ———. *Archaeology and the Religion of Israel*. Baltimore: Johns Hopkins University Press, 1953.
>
> Biran, Avaraham. "House of David." *Biblical Archaeology Review* (March/April 1994).
>
> Brotzman, Ellis. *Old Testament Textual Criticism*. Grand Rapids: Baker, 1994.
>
> Bruce, F. F. *The Books and the Parchments: How We Got Our English Bible*. Old Tappan, NJ: Fleming H. Revell, 1950.
>
> Geisler, Norman. *Christian Apologetics*. Grand Rapids: Baker, 1976.

Geisler, Norman, and William E. Nix. *A General Introduction to the Bible*. Chicago: Moody, 1986.

Horn, Siegfried H. "Recent Illumination of the Old Testament." *Christianity Today* 12 (1968): 13-17.

Kitchen, K. A. *Ancient Orient and the Old Testament*. Downers Grove, IL: InterVarsity, 1966.

McDowell, Josh. *The New Evidence that Demands a Verdict*. Nashville: Thomas Nelson, 1999.

Wilson, Clifford A. *Rocks, Relics, and Biblical Reliability*. Grand Rapids: Zondervan, 1977.

Wilson, Robert Dick. *A Scientific Investigation of the Old Testament*. Chicago: Moody, 1959.

Wiseman, Donald F. "Archaeological Confirmation of the Old Testament." In *Revelation and the Bible*, ed. Carl Henry, 301-16. Grand Rapids: Baker, 1958.

Yamauchi, Edwin. *The Stones and the Scriptures*. Philadelphia: Lippincott, 1972.

Cheers,
Prof. Dave

Exchange 13

I'm Having a Difficult Time Understanding the Christian Notions of Sin and Salvation

Dear Prof,

I had no idea there was so much rich historical and archeological support for the Bible. That truly fascinates me, and I have a lot of reading and studying to do. (I'm beginning to appreciate now why there are seminaries and graduate degrees in religion and theology—this is far more serious and involved than I ever imagined.) One could easily spend a lifetime studying this stuff.

Lately, I've been reading mainly from the New Testament, and I'm really grappling with the Gospels of Mark and John. When I first wrote you a long time ago (I can't believe we are still discussing this stuff, but I am glad we are . . .), what was really on my mind was death. I just don't know what happens after death. If the atheists and materialists are right, then literally nothing happens—which suggests I really don't have much to worry about, so why bother with all this debate about good, bad, heaven, and hell? Yet, my gut tells me differently. Now that I've been discussing these issues with you, reading the Bible, and reading from some of the books you've mentioned, I'm convinced that there is something to all of this theology. I'm brought back to my original underlying questions for which atheism and materialism just don't seem to have clear answers that are intellectually and emotionally satisfying.

By reading through the Gospels and examining what Christ is teaching, it seems clear to me that he is saying man is basically sinful and that the only way to heaven is to believe in him. I remember this distinctly in the Gospel of John. I'm sure it's in the other Gospels, but John stands out in my mind. Okay, so humans are sinful, there is a heaven and a hell, and the only way to heaven is to believe in Jesus Christ. But it doesn't make sense to me that a really bad person, like a mass murderer or someone like Hitler, can at the last minute believe in Jesus and go to heaven, while a basically good, religious person who doesn't truly believe in Jesus will not go to heaven. This doesn't seem right or fair to me. Also, it seems that this salvation through faith in Jesus is potentially like the tenure system for you professors (no offense, ha ha). It's like job security—once you're in you can sit back and do nothing or do a half-ass job and still get paid. It's basically heavenly job security of sorts. I don't mean to be crass or overly sarcastic, but I'm confused about this. It's a real concern for me, and I hope you can help clear it up.

Sincerely,
Seeker

Dear Seeker,

This is an excellent question, and it is a serious stumbling block for many people. I think it may be helpful to start by analyzing the question. I'll begin my answer, as I sometimes do, by asking a question (a discussion strategy Christ himself used quite nicely): could a person like Hitler have ever been a true believer and still do the things he did? The answer is clearly no. If someone truly believes Christ is the Son of God, is the redeemer of humanity, is the one who took upon himself the sins of the world, is the one who took our place on the cross and took the rightful consequences of our sin (death and separation from a pure, holy, and righteous God) so that those who believe would not have to endure this rightful and just punishment, is the one who is thus our savior, if anyone truly believes all these things, that person will naturally also accept Christ as not only savior but also Lord. Thus, for the true believer, Christ is the savior of his/her soul and also the Lord, King, or Sovereign of his/her life. That is, the believer accepts Christ as the one who reconciles him/her to God and also as the one who thus rules over his/her life. The true believer willingly and lovingly submits to a loving and righteous God who, through Christ, died for that believer (expression of his love); and the believer seeks to follow Christ's commands and moral law (the outward expression of his righteousness). That willing submission to this loving and sovereign Lord is reflected in the life of the believer.

Christ said quite simply, "If you love me, you will keep my commands" (John 14:15). Notice, these are not the words of a tyrant. Christ did not say, "Submit or I will crush you like the worm that you are." No. He is commanding us to love him, because he loved us first, so much so that he chose willingly to die in our place so that we might be reconciled to God. When I think of what Christ did for me, let alone for all who believe, and when I think that even though I was his enemy (of my own choosing) and that my sins put him on the cross and that he still loved me (and the world) enough to die for me, how can I not love him? How can I not desire to follow him? How can I not desire to please him? How can I not seek his grace and power to do what he wants me to do?

Because he died for me, I know he is not a tyrant. (Tyrants do not die for others; they kill others for their own selfish sake.) Because he formed my spiritual and physical being, I believe he knows what is best for me and that he wants what is best for me. Because of his great love, he desires only what is good for me. Therefore, I trust that he will not steer me wrong and that his commands are designed for my good. Out of love and awe (the Bible uses the term *fear* here, which means a reverential awe, not an oppressive terror), I willingly submit to his sovereign lordship over my life. I don't always get it right, but as a loving Lord he forgives, teaches, and empowers me toward holiness.

Directly after Jesus said that if we love him we will obey his commands, he then promised to provide help and power to do so through the Holy Spirit: "And I will ask the Father, and he will give you another Helper, to be with you forever, even the Spirit of truth, whom the world cannot receive, because it neither sees him nor knows him. You know him, for he dwells with you and will be in you" (John 14:16–17). What a gracious, loving promise. Christ fills believers with a new love for him, and through this new love and through the aid of the Holy Spirit, the believer willingly chooses to obey Christ's commands. The true believer could not do what Hitler did and also claim to love Christ. These actions and statements are incompatible.

So, my first response is that the mass murderer or the person who commits genocide is not a true believer. Now, I am not God and do not know a person's heart. But, it is not logically possible, based upon Christ's teachings, for the mass murderer who willingly commits such atrocities to also love Christ and be a true believer at the same time. Now, this is not to say that a true believer is without sin. Such a concept is not biblical, nor is it true. Believers in Christ, sadly, still sin. Paul and John, who got their knowledge from Christ, both teach in their letters to the early church (the New Testament epistles) that believers still sin. Once a person believes Christ as Lord and Savior and has a true conversion, that person, in Paul's words, is putting on the new man and is slowly being transformed into the image of Christ (Col 3:5–10). This goes back to the Old Testament teaching that we are made in God's image. But, as a result of sin, that image is damaged and we are separated from God.

Basically, sin is that which misses the mark of God's purity and holiness. Sin is any thought, action, deed, or attitude that violates God's moral law, that goes against his goodness, and that contradicts or speaks contrary to God's truth. Yet out of love, Christ died for us sinners, and those who believe in him experience a gradual process known as sanctification—the process of becoming set apart or different, holy, and pure. The true believer should experience a change in his/her thinking, beliefs, attitudes, actions, speech, and behavior. The true believer should become less sinful and more Christ-like each day. This is one outward indicator of true belief and true salvation.

Again, Christ said, if you love me you will obey my commands. The true believer who has a true conversion experience and now has new thoughts and attitudes inspired by the indwelling of the Holy Spirit also has a new desire, out of love, to please God and to do his will. This process of change is different in different people. Also, there are times of backsliding (as some call it) where a believer seems to move away from Christ. This is where encouragement and discipline from the church or other believers and prodding from the Holy Spirit can help that person get back on the right track; but the person has not lost his/her salvation. Christ is very clear and says that no one and no power can remove from his hand what God has placed there (John 10:28). That means if anyone truly believes, then nothing can remove him/her from God's grace and salvation. The true believer will persevere through many difficulties and challenges, which means he/she will continue to seek after God and to do his will, despite what may happen in his/her life. There may be ups and downs, but overall, the true believer is growing in Christ and seeking to do his will on this earth, all for the glory of God.

Some feel it isn't fair that a person who tries to be good all his life but does not believe in Christ will not go to heaven, while a person who was evil but then has a true conversion before he dies will go to heaven. That doesn't seem fair. Well, let's think about it for a moment.

What is just? What is fair? What ought to happen to everyone? Remember the rich young man in the Gospels who addressed Christ as "good teacher" (Mark 10:17; Luke 18:18)? Christ asked the key question, "Why do you call me good? No one is good except God alone" Mark 10:18). This statement says two things: one, this is another example of Christ asserting that he is God in the flesh. (Only God is good; you recognize me as "good"; therefore, you should recognize me as God.) Christ's second point is relevant to our discussion here. Since only God is good, then no one else is good. And since no one else is good, then no one can stand before God truly and completely blameless. No one.

Indeed, everyone is good compared to some other human being, but no one is good compared to God. God is the standard. So, what is fair is that everyone be banished from God's presence. No one is good enough to be with God, who alone is holy and pure. But, because God loves his creation, he provides for a way to return to his presence. This is his grace. Grace is an undeserved gift. God gives us the undeserved gift of himself in the person of Christ. Through Christ, God sacrificed himself and took upon himself our punishment. If we accept this gracious gift, then we can be in his presence. If we accept this gift and stand before God, God will look at us and will not see our true selves (sinful, impure, unholy, unlike God); rather, he will look upon his believers and will instead see Christ (that is, he will see his own purity and goodness). Only through Christ can we thus stand in God's presence. The "good person" (good as compared to some other worse person) who does not believe in Christ and who has not accepted God's gracious gift is not good enough by his/her own merit. No one alone, using his/her own merit, is good enough.

What is good enough? To be as God. To be good enough, we must be exactly like God. But on our own, we cannot be exactly like God. Only by accepting Christ by faith can we stand in God's presence. Even then, we are not in ourselves good enough. Rather, it is God, through Christ in us, who is good enough. So, the person who tried to do good deeds but never believed in Christ is not good enough. When he stands before God, God sees only the sinful man. No matter how good our deeds are, we are still sinful and the deeds are tainted with that sin. And, all the good deeds that we do cannot erase the fact of our evil deeds. However, the evil person who confessed his sins, accepted Christ as Lord and Savior, and truly repented (meaning he truly turned away from his sinful actions and thoughts) is also not good enough in himself. But, because he believes in Christ, God sees Christ in him, not his sinful being, and he is thus considered good (again, not because he himself is good but because he knows the Son, Jesus Christ, who is God and who is truly good). Christ said, "Whoever has the Son has life; whoever does not have the Son of God does not have life" (1 John 5:12).

So, it isn't really an issue of what is fair, because it is fair that all people be separated from God. Rather, it is a question of what is just and loving. Justice and love are both served through the grace of God. Jesus experienced the consequences of our sin (death and separation from God) in our place. Justice was served. God sacrificed himself through Christ so that those who believe can be reconciled to God. This is love. Through grace (undeserved gift) both God's justice and his love are satisfied. In and of themselves, both the so-called good person and the evil person should perish. Neither is good enough. But, the one who accepts the gift of Christ is saved, because in God's eyes he sees not the sinful person but the image of righteousness in Christ.

My heart breaks at your last question. Indeed, there are some who (wrongly) believe that all they have to do is accept Christ and then they are free to do whatever they want on earth or to do nothing at all with their new life in Christ. This is a dangerous and false notion. Christ never taught such a thing. Christ said, "If you love me, you will keep my commandments" (John 14:15). The saved person is not free to do whatever he wants, nor is he free to do nothing to further the kingdom of God. True salvation means lovingly and willingly submitting to the lordship of Christ, to do his will on this earth. Only a truly saved person will do this. Also, Christ commanded his believers to go out and to make disciples. This means the true believer must share the Gospel (the "good news" of Christ) with others, to tell others about Christ, to teach others the truths of Christ, in the hope that others will also believe in Christ. So, salvation is not like professorial tenure (ha ha), even though some people wrongly treat it as such.

To those who are confused or who have not yet committed to belief in Christ, God says, "Come now, let us reason together" (Isa 1:18). He wants people to come to truth, to come to faith in him. That is why he came to earth in human flesh. That is why he revealed and taught the truth. That is why he died on the cross for human sins. And that is why he rose again from the dead. Think about this: the disciples were directly with Christ for three years. Guess what: they didn't fully get it either at first. Many times, Christ became frustrated with the disciples. Even after so many miracles and authoritative teaching, the disciples wondered, who is this man?

In the Gospel of Mark, Christ finally asks the disciples, "Who do people say that I am?" (8:27). They answered: John the Baptist (Herod had John the Baptist executed and some thought Jesus was John the Baptist resurrected), Elijah, or one of the prophets. Notice that many people today think the same thing, that Jesus was just a good man, a nice teacher, or a prophet. Remember that C. S. Lewis in *Mere Christianity* said that a mere good man or a good teacher would not say what Christ said and would not claim to be God. Lewis notes that Christ is one of the following: liar, lunatic, or Lord. He could not be just a good teacher. If you open your mind and heart to the evidence, the logical conclusion is that Jesus is Lord. Jesus then asked his disciples, "But who do you say that I am?" (Mark 8:29). Peter answered, "You are the Christ" (Mark 8:29). Finally, the disciples were starting to get it. But, even though Christ told them that he would suffer, be persecuted, punished, and killed, and that he would rise again (Luke 9:22), they still didn't get it. When Christ was killed, they thought, "Game over," and hid in fear. Not until they saw the resurrected Christ did they start to get it, and even then, Christ had to teach them, again, going through the Scriptures (our Old Testament) proving to them that he is the Christ (Luke 24:13–27). Then, they finally understood and fully believed. Then, they started preaching the truth of Christ.

What does this mean for us? It means that sometimes we don't always get it at first either. It sometimes takes a while. But, Christ said, seek and you will find, knock and the door will be opened to you (Luke 11:9–10). He wants us to seek him out. He desires that we understand the truth and accept it. But he will not force himself on us. That would not be loving. He has given us enough evidence, enough information, enough truth to trust him and to accept him as Lord and Savior. It is my firm belief that if anyone truly seeks him, he/she will find him (Christ promised as much). My encouragement to you is to pray to Jesus each day: "Jesus, you claimed that if I seek you I will find you. Please open my heart and mind and reveal yourself and your truth to me so that I may believe in you." Then, read the book of Mark. Follow that with the book of John. (I know you mentioned that you have read them, but read them again.) Then read the book of Romans (a letter from Paul to the believers in Rome). Pray every day and read a chapter or two every day. Ask any questions that you have. I will do my best by God's grace to answer them. I firmly believe that God will not refuse the seeking of an honest heart and an open mind

Cheers,
Prof. Dave

Dear Prof,

Okay, what you've written makes a lot of sense, but as I was reading and thinking about these ideas of confessing one's sins and trusting in Jesus for salvation, I couldn't help but think that most people who we imagine as repenting in their last breath are doing it out of *fear*. They're afraid that there *may be* some sort of eternal consequence to a lifetime of sinning, killing, or what have you. A person like that saying, "I'm sorry Jesus, please forgive me!" just before he dies isn't really doing it with any conviction other than out of the selfish urge to continue his own existence. Sure, he acknowledges Jesus as God but he only does it because he was scared of dying. How do you respond to this issue?

But the main issue I struggle with is the eternal justice aspect of sin and horrible crimes. Where is the justice against this raving maniac who kills hundreds of people throughout his life and then gets off scot-free because one of the only books he was allowed to read in jail was the Bible and he eventually came to know the Lord at the last minute? I always thought murder is a mortal sin and that there is no getting out of that one. Aren't you doomed if you commit murder, especially if you do it a hundred times, eat the corpses, let the scraps rot, and then fornicate with them? I don't care if the psychopathic murderer finds Jesus on his deathbed; he needs moral and eternal punishment for his sins (at least in my opinion). I understand that God loves his creation and wants us to love him back, but where is his wrath with respect to such a sick individual, this disgrace of God's creation? Where's the divine justice? What price does the psycho pay? Nothing?

Wow, I'm really riled up here, and I'm not sure why. I think there is something in my gut saying, "Wait a minute, it doesn't seem fair that the horrific murderer who accepts Christ just gets off scot-free."

Sincerely,
Seeker

Dear Seeker,

Wow! We seem to have hit a spiritual nerve, so to speak. That's okay. Let's try to sort it out. Indeed, some people on death row may make a panic decision out of mere self-interest that isn't totally sincere. Yet, others may make true, honest, and sincere decisions to accept Christ as God and Savior. But, let's be honest with ourselves: what decision for Christ is not about keeping ourselves from suffering the pain of being separated from God eternally? Aren't we all in one way or another concerned about the eternal state of our existence? Aren't we all scared of dying, regardless if we know when it is coming (the person on death row) or not (the average Joe working nine to five)? Can we really say that the death-row or deathbed conversion is necessarily any less sincere than the decision made after months or even years of study, contemplation, and prayer? The Holy Spirit can make someone keenly aware of his/her sinful and condemned spiritual condition at any time. Maybe it took a severe illness or a life of crime to finally get through to that person on his/her deathbed or on death row. We just don't know the divine purposes of God. Our minds are too finite to know all of the historical ramifications for why things happen the way they do, but God in his infinite wisdom does know all of the historical ramifications of any one single act, from World War II to the planting of a seed in your garden. God uses many instances, good and bad, beautiful and horrific, to bring about his desired will. I don't think we are in a place to judge the difference between a deathbed conversion and any other conversion. A rational decision made after years of contemplation can be just as insincere as a hasty one made before certain death; conversely, a hasty, last-minute decision can also be just as powerfully sincere and true as a sincere decision made after years of contemplation. The Holy Spirit reaches different people with the truth in different ways.

I sympathize with your other follow-up question, which basically addresses the matter of justice. You mention murder as a mortal sin with the suggestion, I think, that such a sin is unforgivable and that the murderer cannot escape the condemnation of that sin. Christ said that the only unforgivable sin is blasphemy against the Holy Spirit or God. He made this statement when some Jewish leaders accused him of being of Satan, and said that his powers of healing were of the devil (Matt 12:31–32 and Mark 3:22–30). There are a few ways theologians view this issue of the one unforgivable sin declared by Christ (that of blasphemy against the Holy Spirit). Here is one perspective, and the logic here is quite simple: The only path to forgiveness according to Christ as revealed in his teachings and recorded in the Gospels is accepting Christ as God and Savior. But, if you reject him then you cannot ever be forgiven, because you are rejecting the only means of forgiveness. This rejection of Christ is unforgivable and you are trapped in an eternal sin, because denying Christ keeps you from ever receiving God's forgiveness. Again: the person rejecting Christ traps himself. God will not forgive anyone who rejects him because the person rejects the very source of the forgiveness itself. You see the dilemma? God is the only one who can forgive sin against God. How can you be forgiven by that which you deny and reject? But, any other sin (murder, for example) can be forgiven if the person accepts Christ and his forgiveness. So, as horrific as murder is, it is not an eternal, unforgivable sin. Only the utter rejection of God and his complete nature and being is unforgivable (as explained above). But, if someone were to renounce his rejection of God and come to faith in God through Christ, then there is forgiveness, because the source of forgiveness is finally acknowledged and accepted.

But wait a minute, I hear you asking, what about justice? What about punishment? Isn't the murderer who truly accepts Christ right before his death getting off scot-free? In the spiritual sense—Yes! Now, before you jump through your computer screen (ha ha), let's not forget that this murderer on death row has not escaped all justice—there is a degree of earthly, punitive justice. He was caught, tried, found guilty, and sentenced according to the laws of the land (in the United States, imprisonment and, in your scenario, capital punishment). So, there is justice. Also, we can experience a level of justice for our sins and crimes by enduring the various natural and legal consequences of our sins—we may experience personal losses, broken relationships, financial ruin, physical deterioration, emotional crisis, and so on. There are often degrees of negative consequences that we suffer in our lives brought on by sins we commit ourselves (be they hidden or exposed). Furthermore, those who sin (which, by the way is everyone) and who never accept Christ as God and Savior are eternally separated from God, who is holy and pure. This separation is justice.

However, those who believe in Jesus Christ, though they are sinners, will get off scot-free, as you say, by the grace of God. Where's the justice in this? The justice is served via the substitutionary death of Christ on the cross. Again, it is important to remember that we all deserve physical and spiritual death. We all deserve to be eternally separated from the relational presence of God. No one deserves to be in his glorious presence. The whole point of God's self-sacrifice through Christ is so that those who believe may be spared the eternal punishment that is our due—so that those who believe may get off scot-free (to use your phrase). God, through Christ, took our punishment and thus served justice for us. So, justice is still served. There still is the right and just punishment for sin. Christ experienced it all.

That's why I am humbled before the throne of grace and the majesty of Christ. I get off scot-free only because God, through Christ, suffered what I was supposed to suffer (the right and just punishment for my sins—separation from God). Here we see love (self-sacrifice), combined with justice (God's wrath poured out on Christ who took it in our place), expressed through grace (God's gift to us even though we do not deserve it). How can I not love and serve this glorious God? I cannot be upset that the reformed and truly repentant murderer does not get punished by separation from God, because I too should be similarly punished for my sins. The fact that God, through Christ, paid my penalty and the penalty of all who believe fills me with wonder and awe at the boundless love of God.

Not only is there justice, but there is also justification. By dying in our stead, God serves justice, and he also justifies the sinner who believes. Through faith in Christ, we are justified (made right with God) in God's eyes. This is cause for wonderment and celebration. We all have a deep-seated desire to see justice done, and this desire is more evidence of a moral absolute, for which the absolute God is the source. But, we should be careful when we call for eternal justice on those we perceive as worse sinners than ourselves. I know you are a fan of *The Lord of the Rings*. Remember how Frodo was so upset that Bilbo showed grace to Gollum and let him live? Gandalf then asked Frodo if he were so righteous and wise as to determine who should live and who should die. The point here is theological: we are not so holy and wise ourselves as to be able to determine such things. We all deserve eternal punishment for our sins. Praise God that He loved us enough to die, through Christ, in our place. That grace is available to all who believe.

Cheers,
Prof. Dave

Dear Prof,

I'm following you pretty well when we keep the discussion about the hypothetical serial murderer or really bad people, but in your last message, you used a lot of *we* and *us* pronouns. This makes me really uncomfortable. If I'm reading this correctly, you are basically saying I'm a bad or sinful person and deserve to be separated from God. But how can this be? I'm not such a bad person as all that. And, what if I became a religious person and did good works? Doesn't that make me different than a sinful person? Won't my good works make me right with God? That makes sense to me.

Sincerely,
Seeker

Dear Seeker,

As hard as it may be to accept, deeds and mere religion will not grant you access to the presence of God. Only the grace of God can do that. Don't get me wrong: actions are important, but only in so far as they are serving God's will. Actions do not save us. The believer will desire to do God's will, and he relies on the strength of Christ to empower him to do God's will. But, the amount of good works will not determine your path into heaven, and the amount of evil deeds will not determine your path to hell. All people, in and of themselves, are already separated from God by the sin nature. We all like to think that we are pretty good, but compared to whom? (Recall the earlier part of this exchange.) God is the ultimate standard. Can anyone really say that he/she is good enough? Can any one of us really claim that our good works will be enough to merit being in the presence of a holy and righteous God? Think of it this way: imagine a huge room, and pasted on the walls of this room you see every thought, action, deed, feeling, and statement you ever made in your entire life. Would you want anyone to see that—your mother or your father or your best friend? I know I wouldn't.

Now, would you want God to see it? Well, he does. Deep down, we all know that on our own merit we can never be good enough to stand in his holy and righteous presence. Some may think that they have more good than bad, so that is good enough. Yet, we can never really have more good than bad, because even our best actions are tainted by our sin nature. But, let's just grant for the sake of argument a scenario in which a person has more good deeds than bad ones. So, he comes before God with a big pile of good deeds and (for argument's sake) a smaller pile of bad deeds. Now, this person is hoping that the good will outweigh or balance out the bad. But God would look at both piles, and what is still present? The bad. Regardless of how much good there is, this good does not erase the bad. The bad still exists, and as long as it exists it keeps this person from God's relational presence. That is why Christ (his life, death, and resurrection) is necessary. Faith in Christ overshadows the bad in us, such that when the believer stands before God, God sees Christ overshadowing the bad, just as if the bad did not exist. God will look at the believer and see Christ. Thus, through faith in Christ the believer can have a relationship with God and be in his eternal presence.

Note that religious devotion or being religious will not save us. Christ said as much to the Jewish leaders of the first century (Matt 23). They were all concerned about following rules and regulations, and they forgot about God. Christ called them hypocrites, which in the Greek means those who wear masks. They were religious on the outside and followed all the rules, but their hearts were dark and sinful. Christ taught that the problem we have is a heart problem. We are sinful. Good deeds and religious acts will not correct our sinful hearts. Only through faith in Christ will our sin and heart issues be properly dealt with.

A good example is racism. We can pass all the external laws we want, but that will not take care of the internal problem of racism. (I'm not saying we should not have racial discrimination laws; I'm just saying that a legal code against racism will not erase racism.) Racism is a matter of the heart, and to deal with racism we must deal with the heart. Only by changing the heart will we change racism. Christ changes hearts. Now, again, don't get me wrong. Being religious can be a good thing, as long as it does not become hypocrisy, as long is it doesn't replace faith in Christ. Religious practice can be a helpful way to nurture your relationship with Christ, but the most important thing is having a relationship with Christ, not mere religiosity. Relationship with Christ is fostered by reading the Bible, discussing issues with other believers, worshiping God, and fellowshiping with believers by attending church. Note, attending church or reading the Bible in themselves will not save a person. But, church attendance and reading the Bible can lead a person to a relationship with Christ and then help that person grow in Christ and become the person God wants him to be.

Cheers,
Prof. Dave

Dear Prof,

This is pretty heavy, and I think I may be a little confused. You say that God is all pure and holy and that no one deserves to be in his presence because all have sinned. But God knows that the earth is full of sin, so what are we supposed to do? Doesn't he want to be rejoined with his creation, no matter how bad we are, the way a mother still loves and desires to see her son even while he's in jail for robbing a convenience store?

Sincerely,
Seeker

Dear Seeker,

Indeed, God does love us despite our sin, far more than the human mother loves her criminal son. But we must remember who we are in relation to this God of love, justice, and holiness. No one deserves to be in God's presence because we have messed things up through our sin. Humans were not made sinful. According to the Bible, God made Adam and Eve perfect and good. But, he also made them free and thus with the potential to sin (but not the inevitability of sinning). Because they chose freely to sin, they became sinful. Because like begets like, a sinful Adam and Eve begot sinful offspring. We are all now by nature sinful and we sin. Therefore, we deserve death and separation from God (this is the just consequence of sin, as we already discussed). The issue is not what are *we* to do, because we really can do nothing. The mother of the convict still wants to see her son, but she recognizes that justice should be served as well. How much more so with God! God longs for his creatures to be with him, but he must be true to himself and have justice served. The question, then, becomes, what is *he* to do?

The answer is that he has done it all. Given that his creatures freely messed everything up and cursed themselves, what could God do? To serve justice, he could let us all perish as we deserve. Although this would express his justice, it would not express his divine love. God acts in accordance with his complete divine nature, so how is he to achieve justice *and* love? He sacrificed himself through Christ to save his creatures. In this act, there is both justice and love. This is how we are reconciled to him. The key point here is that all of God's qualities must be satisfied: righteousness, justice, mercy, and love. All of this is satisfied through God's grace, his gift of himself through Christ. Since we could not save ourselves, he saved us through the death of Christ on the cross. All who freely and sincerely believe that Christ is God and Savior are forgiven and reconciled to God. Those who believe also lovingly and willingly submit to his lordship in their lives; they pick up their cross and follow him out of a new love and desire to honor him.

I know this is really weighty stuff, and I hope that I have helped a little bit. I recommend that you keep reading the Gospels and Romans (this is the Apostle Paul's letter to believers in Rome during the first century, and in it he explains the problem of humanity's sin, God's righteous condemnation of sinners, and salvation through faith in Christ). I also highly recommend John Stott's *The Cross of Christ*. It is not a quick read, because it is extremely thorough and detailed. Stott outlines the issues very clearly, and he provides in-depth discussions. Even though this book is serious theology, I think it will be accessible to you, and I highly recommend it.

Cheers,
Prof. Dave

Exchange 14

What about Those Who Never Hear about Christ?

Dear Prof,

That was some exchange we had. I'm sorry for not writing sooner, but that was pretty intense, and I'm still trying to sort it all out. I also finally got a copy of Stott's book and am trying to read it. It's pretty serious, and it addresses in much more detail many of the things we discussed recently. Thanks for recommending it.

I was listening to some friends the other day who were none too thrilled with the Christian idea of Christ being the only way to God. They found it rather distasteful and thought that such a view is horribly narrow-minded and that it presents an arbitrary and capricious God who only saves a few here and there who happen to hear about Christ and believe in him. That really got me to thinking, and so I have another question. Let's just say, for example, that an indigenous man from a remote island off the coast of Africa lived his life almost sin free. Maybe his tribe permits him to have multiple wives or something, but other than that, he has given away every bit of wealth he has accumulated, given up his home to others in the tribe who need it, and practiced numerous other Christ-like good deeds throughout his lifetime. However, he was never exposed to the Bible and never learned about Christ. Does this mean he's not allowed in heaven because he never learned to read? Is he not allowed in heaven because his remote island was cut off from society and he never learned about Christ? Shouldn't his deeds count for something? There are many people like this in the world, I should think. It just doesn't seem fair that such people are not allowed into heaven.

Sincerely,
Seeker

Dear Seeker,

I'm so glad you are finding the Stott book helpful. I really like that book a lot. Please keep reading it. Some sections may get dense, but just do your best. Hang in there with it, and I'm sure you'll be blessed for your efforts.

Hah, I was wondering when this question would come up. It's a tough one, but there are good answers. I pray your heart and mind are open to consider the answers thoughtfully and carefully. Let's note right off the bat that a person is never rejected by God because of race, geography (i.e., location of birth), education level, or illiteracy. Rather, God rightly rejects a person in response to that person's sin. In fact, the Bible tells us in the book of Romans (3:23) that all people have sinned and fallen short of the glory of God (that is, we in no way on our own rank up there with God, and we cannot on our own meet God's standard for purity which only he can meet). The book of Romans (6:23) also tells us that the wages of sin is death; that is, because of sin, we have no right to be in the presence of God who is totally sinless, pure, and righteous, and thus we should all be cut off from God's presence—this is death. In this regard, all people are treated equally before God. All people deserve death. All people deserve to be cut off from a holy and pure God. The question, then, is what's to be done about it? (I'll give you a hint: the glorious solution is provided in the verses following the serious verses given above; namely, the solution is found the grace of God alone, as stated in Romans 3:24 and the second part of Romans 6:23.)

Some approach this dilemma from the perspective of deeds, which you seem to be doing as well. You asked if the hypothetical indigenous man's deeds count for anything. Sure, deeds count for something, but the real question is, do they count toward a person's salvation? The answer is no. Why not? Let's ask the question differently. Can your good deeds make you equivalent in holiness and purity to God? No. Remember a few months ago in an earlier exchange we were talking about this issue of deeds or merit in salvation? Remember that the standard for who is good enough is God himself. In order to be in the presence of God, we must be pure like him. Jesus clearly and directly said, "You therefore must be perfect as your heavenly Father is perfect" (Matt 5:48). God gave us the moral law to show us what it means to be morally good. The Ten Commandments are a great summary of this moral law (Exod 20:1–17). Can you honestly say that you (or anyone else, except Jesus Christ himself) has lived a lifetime and never violated a single one of the Ten Commandments? That's the basic test. Ever tell a simple lie? Ever steal anything (even a small thing like a pencil or piece of paper)? You don't have to commit any of the biggies, just one teensy tiny lie and you are no longer equivalent with God in terms of moral purity.

Now, there is also the notion of original sin which says all humans are born sinful, and thus our sinful natures in themselves make us not equivalent to God in terms of moral purity. So, just from this idea alone, no one can ever stand before God on his or her own merit and claim to be morally equivalent with him. No one is good enough to stand in the presence of God. No one. Remember the room illustration we discussed in an earlier e-mail exchange? Imagine a room in which there are pictures on the wall of every thought, statement, and action you ever committed in your life. Everything is on the walls, the good, the bad, and the ugly! Would you want anyone to see that room? Probably not. I know I wouldn't want anyone to see my wall. I think that illustration puts it in perspective. We are not good enough on our own merit to warrant being let into heaven, as you put it. We cannot earn our way into heaven. No matter how many good deeds we do, they do not erase the presence of the evil deeds.

The existence of the evil in our lives (sin) prohibits us from being with God. That is why we need a savior. And this is where the grace or the gift of God comes into play, the grace mentioned in Romans 3:24 and in the last part of Romans 6:23. God is our savior through the person of Jesus Christ. God graciously paid the penalty for our sins through the person of Christ who lived a sinless life, died on the cross as atonement for sin, and rose again, triumphant over death. Only by faith in Jesus Christ can we stand in the presence of God, as I've explained in earlier e-mail messages. Your friends say this is narrow-minded and distasteful. Well, they are entitled to their view, but just remember that this truth is not merely my opinion. This is precisely what Jesus himself taught. So, if your friends don't like the idea, they must take it up with Christ. It is the truth proclaimed by Christ, who very clearly said, "I am the way, and the truth, and the life. No one comes to the Father except through me" (John 14:6). Jesus did not say he was one of many ways. He said he was *the* way. What he said is not an idea made up by later Christians, nor is it merely an opinion of some Christians. It is the truth of God as taught by Jesus Christ.

Now, back to your question about those who never hear about Jesus Christ. This question is one that most skeptics hold onto as justification for their rejection of Christ's teaching. In my opinion, that will be flimsy ground upon which to stand before God and say, "I rejected you because I didn't receive what I considered to be a satisfactory answer to this question about the individual who may never have heard about Christ or read the Bible." To which God will simply say, lovingly, "That's fine, but you are not that person. You have heard of me and my son. What is your excuse?" I think this is a key point. When you stand before God, the issue will not be what did those who never heard about Jesus think about God but, rather, what do you, who *did* hear about Jesus and had access to the Bible, believe about God and his son Jesus Christ? God will not ask you what others said and believed. He will ask you what did *you* think and believe. You must account for yourself. Please keep that in mind.

The way this question (or objection, really) is phrased assumes that God is somehow unfair and unjust. But is he really? Since we know that everyone sins and that no one is holy and pure like God because of our sin nature, then it is just, fair, and right that everyone should perish. This may sound harsh, because in today's culture we are not used to hearing such things, but this statement is by definition fair and just. No one is good enough, so it is *fair* that everyone be separated from a good, holy, and pure God. Justice is often harsh, and we consider it harshest when justice is measured against ourselves. We would all like to be pardoned when we are stopped for speeding on the highway. But, we know that the cop is under no obligation whatsoever to pardon us or to let us go with a warning. Justice demands that we be given a ticket. How grateful we are when we are pardoned, but we have no right to demand that we be pardoned. The same is true for people's relationship with God. No matter who you are or where you are from, no one deserves to be pardoned and no one can demand pardon. God's pardon through Christ is an unwarranted gift. It is grace. Grace cannot be demanded. Grace is freely given. As such, God is under no obligation to save everyone, let alone anyone. (Please ponder this last sentence, for it is key to this lengthy answer.)

This strict justice does not necessarily make God cruel, unfair, or discriminatory. No. He is perfectly justified in letting everyone perish, for that is what justice demands. Ah, but since God is loving and merciful as well as just and righteous, he does provide a way back to him through the gracious gift of Christ. Out of love and mercy, he does provide such grace. In his divine wisdom, he has provided this grace into the world as he has created it, in the best possible way so that the most people possible can experience that grace. His creatures are material and spiritual (we are souls in a physical body), so his grace must be expressed in body and spirit (in the person of Christ). The universe God created is bound within time, so his grace to individuals in this universe has been expressed within time. That is the basic story line of the Bible. It is the story of God's creation, the fall of his creation (by human's sinful actions), and God's unfolding within history his extensive plan of salvation, culminating in Jesus Christ and the establishment of the church in the first century. So, I believe that God in his infinite wisdom has expressed his grace in the best possible way given the nature of the universe he has created and in which we live.

Ultimately, God became man, in Christ, and lived in time, in a geographical area, during a time in history when it was most possible for people to apprehend the message and the grace and to spread it as quickly as possible to the known world. It's no accident that Christ came to Palestine during the Roman occupation when there was a common language through which the message (the Gospel of Jesus Christ) could be spread to the greatest number of people possible. Moreover, God continues to use his believers in time and through history to spread his truth so that more may experience this grace. Therefore, God is neither unfair nor unjust in his choice to express his grace. Again, by definition, grace does not obligate God to anything or anyone. Grace is an undeserved gift, given freely by a loving God. He is free to give it to no one, to a single person, or to as many people as possible within the limitations of the physical universe as he created it.

Also note that God is neither arbitrary nor capricious. He planned this grace from the very beginning. He didn't think it up later. He knew exactly what would happen in his creation, and he always already had a plan of salvation. He unfolded his plan of gracious salvation in history, over time, through the Jewish people, whom he chose for his own reasons according to his own divine wisdom and for his own glory to be the agents of his salvation. He revealed his plan to the people through the Old Testament prophets, and he accomplished exactly what he planned to do and what he revealed through these prophets. Nothing arbitrary there. Nothing capricious. He chose to offer salvation out of his love and for his glory. Indeed, what a blessing for us, and I'm thankful he chose to do so.

What about that person who never hears about Christ or reads the Bible? On the one hand, I simply don't know. I am not God. I cannot know the full mind of God. I can only know that which he chose to reveal to us in his word, the Bible. I trust in a loving, merciful, just, and holy God. I trust that anything he does is right, good, and just. The Bible teaches that for salvation, people need to learn about Christ and to accept him as Lord and Savior. That is why Christ calls upon his believers to spread the Gospel, so that as many people as possible may learn of Christ. This is the purpose of missions. Jesus Christ himself commanded that all believers should go out and make disciples of Christ (this is known as the Great Commission as stated in Matt 28:19–20). That is, all believers must teach this truth, this Gospel, to others. Christians didn't make up the idea of missions. Christ commanded it. And, Christ said if we truly love him, then we will obey his commands (John 14:15). So, the Christian tells others about Christ. Many skeptics often criticize the Christian for the problem of the person who never hears about Jesus (saying it is problematic because not everyone will hear the Gospel), yet these same skeptics also criticize the Christian for mission work and for trying to spread the Gospel. What does the skeptic want or expect? You cannot blame the Christian for this problem and then also criticize the Christian for working to resolve the problem.

God also knows the true hearts of all people. I firmly believe that if there is someone in a remote area whom God knows would indeed accept Christ only if he were to hear of Christ, then God will make it possible for that person to somehow hear about Christ. There are many examples of nonbelievers who recognize that there is a God, that they are impure, and that they need a mediator to reconcile them to this God. For example, in one of his many lectures, Ravi Zacharias tells of a certain missionary to Indonesia in the late nineteenth or early twentieth century who went there and suffered great hardship, lost his wife and children, but continued to work there, translating the Bible into the indigenous language. After his death, it was revealed that the local people had a prophecy, which this missionary did not know about, which spoke of a strange man coming from a strange land with a truth that they needed to hear, and that this man would translate this truth to them. So, here is a great example of God revealing to unbelievers that there is a truth they will receive and need to hear, and God fulfilled that prophecy through this missionary. There are also reports that people who never heard of Christ dreamed about Christ and came to believe in him with the aid of later being exposed to the Gospel. There have been reports of Muslims being convinced of the truth of Christ by visions and dreams and then seeking out Christians to learn about the Gospel. Christ taught that God is seeking those who desire to worship him in spirit and truth (John 4:23). I have faith that God honors such seekers by providentially acting in their lives to get the Gospel to them.

This is indeed a difficult issue that is not easily resolved. There is much theological debate on this point as well. However, I have presented what I think is a reasonable answer to the question. As I learn more I may be able to revise and clarify my view. But, regardless of what happens to the person who never hears about Christ (again, I leave such people to the infinite mercy and wisdom of a just and righteous God), the real question is: who do *you* say Christ is? Just because a person has not heard of Christ does not excuse the person who *has* heard about Christ. God will deal justly, fairly, and mercifully with those who do not hear the Gospel. He will also deal with us, those who have heard about Christ. We need to worry about us and not allow our concern or confusion or indignation about a seemingly unanswered question to interfere with our decision about Christ. Christ asked his disciples, "Who do the people say that I am?" He then asked them, "Who do you say that I am?" (Luke 9:18–20). When we stand before God, he will not ask us what the person who never heard the Gospel thinks about Christ. He will ask us, who do you say Christ is? Our individual answer to that question is what counts.

There are two books written by the philosopher and theologian Paul Copan that you may find helpful in exploring these issues further: *True for You, but Not for Me* (1998) and *That's Just Your Interpretation* (2001). I hope this helps a bit.

Cheers,
Prof. Dave

Exchange 15

With All This Sin in the World Caused by Us, Does That Mean God Failed and Let His World Get Out of Control?

Dear Prof,

How's it going? I'm sorry that I haven't written in a while, but I've really been thinking a lot about our last exchange. That was intense. Some things are clicking, other things not, but overall, I'd say it's starting to make sense. I don't know if I agree with it all just yet, but it does make sense. As I was rereading our last few exchanges, I noticed how central the issue of sin is to these discussions. That seems to be the major problem. Sin. I was talking to some friends about all this, particularly the issue of sin. We started to list the various sins and evils we see in the world, and we became a bit discouraged. You keep talking about God who created this world, but is it really his world or not? I'm starting to think that it is not, that he just let it slip away. Why did he do that? That's like me losing control of my bedroom (which, I admit, does happen from time to time, ha ha) or just letting my car run down for lack of care. I take pride in my things, so I don't let them fall apart. If I can keep my things in control, couldn't God do the same with his creation? Doesn't God take pride in us? Sure, he did so enough to give and sacrifice his only son. But, I try to *prevent* my things from needing help later. It's like a vaccine versus a cure. Vaccines are better. They *prevent* you from becoming ill. I prefer preventative maintenance over taking care of my possession or creation *after* the said creation goes bad or falls apart. It seems we humans now need nonstop maintenance. Looking around at things as they are—it seems like it's Satan's world, and it looks as though Satan kicked God's butt.

Sincerely,
Seeker

Dear Seeker,

Hey, it's really good to hear from you. I figured you had a lot to think about with that last exchange. We really covered a lot of information, and I hope you will continue to review it. I'm also excited to learn that you are talking to some of your friends about these issues. Please do share our exchanges with them, and encourage them to read the resources I've mentioned. You all are also welcome to speak to me in person. We can go to a coffee shop and hash some of these issues out over a *café au lait* (or two or three . . .). Since the last few exchanges were marathons, I'll try to keep this one a bit short. I think you still have some thinking and reading to do, but let me address your main concerns here as briefly as possible.

I can sympathize with your reaction. But, I encourage us not to think that God has been defeated, because that is the exact deception that Satan wants us to believe. Remember when you read in Genesis, chapter 3, how Satan deceived Eve by asking her if God really said she would die if she ate that fruit? His strategy was to get her to doubt God. He is now saying to us, "Is God really in control as he claims to be?" Satan wants us to doubt God, too. One way to think through your question is to consider that God could have created any number of realities: he could have chosen not to create anything at all; he could have created a world in which there was no good or evil, just a reality with no moral compass or direction at all (I find this option to be quite frightening, since there would be no real way to determine the legitimacy or rightness of any action whatsoever); he could have created a world in which we were all forced to love him and to be good (but in this reality there would be no true freedom and thus no true love, because remember love is a choice of the will, and with no freedom of choice there can be no true love); or, he could have created a world that was originally good in which there is free will to choose the good or the bad (and thus the actuality of true love), with the possibility of evil (evil would enter via a free choice). In his wisdom he created the latter. This is the world we see now. Evil entered the world through a choice to go against the moral law of God. Evil is the consequence of this choice.

But, your question still remains. Did God fail? Did God just let the world fall to pieces? Has God really just turned his back and removed his hands from this world? I think not. God has allowed for the moral consequences of choices, thus allowing evil to enter into creation. But, he has not given up on the world or totally removed his sovereign control. God does remove his blessings in a limited sense, allowing us to experience the consequences of our actions. We see this, for example, throughout the Old Testament histories. When the nation of Israel or other nations decided to go it alone or to do things their own way, God let them. He also allowed them to experience the consequences of that choice.

In Psalm 139, King David proclaims the omniscience, omnipotence, and omnipresence of God. That is, God is in control of all things, and nothing escapes his knowledge, wisdom, or plans. This gives the believer much comfort, knowing that even though things can get pretty rough on earth, God is ultimately in control, working all things to his purposes, for the good of his people, and for his glory. In the New Testament, Paul reminds believers, "And we know that for those who love God all things work together for good, for those who are called according to his purpose" (Romans 8:28). Paul also reminds us that God created all things and sustains all things, for reality continues to exist because of God: "for 'in him we live and move and have our being'" (Acts 17:28). Thus without God or if God removed his hand from us, we would not live and not move and not exist. In other words, God is sovereign, or supreme ruler over the universe.

In the Book of Psalms, King David exclaims, "The Lord has established his throne in the heavens, and his kingdom rules over all" (Psalm 103:19). Thus, as sovereign over his creation, he is in control, and he rules according to all of his attributes: righteousness, goodness, justice, love, mercy, and wisdom. We do not always understand all that he allows to happen, but given the totality of his divine nature, we can trust that he rules divinely, and that all he does serves a divinely good purpose that ultimately brings him glory. We see only a tiny snapshot of all reality (past, present, and future), but God knows all things instantaneously and simultaneously. God is in total control, and thus there is a reason and a purpose for all things that happen and exist.

So, God is indeed maintaining the world and the universe. If he truly went away, all would be destroyed. You noted that you prefer prevention versus maintenance. Your statement assumes that God is not interested in prevention and just lets his creation run down. I do not think this is accurate. Remember, human beings are very different than your bedroom. Your bedroom is not a living, free, moral agent. God made humans in his own image, and part of this means that we are free, moral agents. Thus, he allows us to make choices, but also he allows us to experience the consequences of our choices (good and bad). Also note that God did not just let us go without any guidance at all. That would be cruel. Rather, he gave us the moral law as a protective, preventative measure, so to speak. If we choose to violate that moral law, then we must suffer the consequences. But—and this is a most glorious "but"—in addition to prevention (which we are free to accept or not), he also provided the cure for the consequences of sin in the person of Jesus Christ, the Messiah and Savior, as we've discussed previously.

Concerning the power and seeming victory of Satan in this world: in 2 Corinthians 4:4, Paul refers to Satan as the "god of this world," meaning he is a usurper of the fallen world who blinds people to the truth of Christ and the light of God. Remember, though, that God is sovereign over the universe, and that includes Satan. Thus, God is allowing Satan to run amok in the world, for now, and God in his infinite wisdom does so for particular divine purposes. So, Satan has not kicked God's butt, not by a long shot. Satan's defeat was already established from the very beginning of time, prophesied in Genesis 3:15. Christ is the one who will bruise the head of the serpent; he is the one who defeats Satan in the end. Note how the demons who possessed different people acted when they encountered Christ. (See, for example, Matthew 8:28–32.) The demons became immediately fearful of Christ the victor and cried out for mercy. They knew who Christ was, even when the humans did not. These demons were once angels, who were with God, and they know his power, and they know the victory to come in the person of Christ (the second person of the Trinity). They know that he has already won. That is the great message and our hope. We see that victory in the resurrection of Christ.

Moreover, in the visions of John recorded in the book of Revelation, we see the final victory of God over Satan. God allows Satan to act, ultimately, for God's divine purposes. Consider Job. Satan had to ask God for permission to torment Job (he was not free to do so without God's sovereign permission). Satan thought he could win by turning Job against God (just as he hoped to defeat God by corrupting humanity). God allowed

Satan to do his best, and Satan failed, thus learning who is really in control. Simultaneously, God taught Job (and us) about faith in the wisdom and power of God. God is sovereign and is in control, and he allows certain things to occur according to his divine purpose and plan. Sometimes we can see why, other times we cannot, because we are limited, but he is infinite in wisdom and is surprised by nothing, since he ordains and allows all things, again, for his divine purposes, for his glory, and, ultimately, for the good of those who love God.

Is this world fallen? Yes. Is there evil in this world? Yes. Is sin a problem in this world? Yes. Does this mean God has failed or is defeated? No. God's plan of salvation for man and his victory over Satan, evil, and sin were established from the very beginning. Because we are creatures bound by time, we witness this plan unfolding in our time. But for God, victory has always already happened; victory has always already been achieved. This is the wondrous hope of the Christian, and it is a hope based upon the truth as revealed by God in his word, the Bible.

Here are some books that will help you better understand the divine nature of God and his sovereignty:

Carson, D. A. *How Long, O Lord?: Reflections on Suffering Evil.* 2nd ed. Grand Rapids: Baker Academic, 2006.

Guinness, Os. *Unspeakable: Facing Up to the Challenge of Evil.* New York: HarperOne, 2006.

Packer, J. I. *Evangelism and the Sovereignty of God.* Downers Grove, IL: InterVarsity, 1991.

———. *Knowing God.* Downers Grove, IL: InterVarsity, 1993.

Sproul, R. C. *The Holiness of God.* 2nd ed. Carol Stream, IL: Tyndale House, 1998.

Tozer, A. W. *Knowledge of the Holy: The Attributes of God.* New York: HarperCollins, 1978.

Cheers,
Prof. Dave

Exchange 16

For Free Will to Be Actual, Isn't God Required to Be a Manipulative Tester of Wills?

Dear Prof,

    I've noticed that the issue of free will has come up in some of our exchanges. I've also noticed this concept coming up in my philosophy classes and even in some of my biology classes. I sometimes get confused about what free will is and if we even have it or not. But, let's just grant for our discussion's sake the concept of free will, that humans do have a will and a rational mind with which to make choices, and that humans are free, to some extent at least, to reason things out and to make choices. Now, you mentioned in your previous e-mail that Adam and Eve had a choice to follow or not to follow God's moral law, and that because of their choice to disobey, they fell into sin and thus the rest of humanity is now sinful. This makes some sense. I don't know if I agree, but it does in itself make some sense. However, I got to thinking the other day. For free will to be real, to be actual (as my philosophy professor says), there would have to be a scenario in which Adam and Eve were presented with a true moral choice, the consequences of which would determine the outcome for the rest of humanity. If this is the case, doesn't that make God, basically, a sadistic overlord? Isn't he just a manipulative tester of wills, tricking his creation into sin? Would this make God, in some sense, thus ultimately responsible for evil?

Sincerely,
Seeker

Dear Seeker,

Oh, my! You *do* come up with some doozies. To play off the slant of your question, maybe God is using you to test my patience and will. Just kidding! This is a fair question, and it does follow, to some extent, from the direction of our discussions. I sense some other ideas and concerns informing this question, so let me see if I can tease some of these things out and provide a satisfactory answer along the way. As always, I'll do my best.

God did not create evil, nor is evil eternally coexistent with the Good. This latter concept is also known as ethical dualism, and it is not logically sound. Quite simply, if something is eternal, universal, and absolute, then it cannot lack anything. Good and evil are clearly different things, and different things are distinguished from each other by difference (seems obvious on the face of it, but you'd be surprised how many people don't actually realize this). One thing is different from another thing because it has or lacks things that the other has or lacks. For example, a green apple is not the same thing as a red apple because one has redness and the other does not, and one has greenness and the other does not. It is a logical contradiction to say that good is absolute and eternal and that evil is also absolute and eternal. An eternal, absolute thing cannot lack anything in itself. Therefore, you cannot logically posit two different eternal absolute things, because since the two things are different, one or both must lack something of the other; therefore, one or both cannot be eternal and absolute. For this reason (and other reasons, but this is enough for our purposes), Christian theism rejects ethical dualism. It understands God (via his own self-revelation in Scripture) as being absolutely and eternally good. Since God is eternally and absolutely good, he cannot be evil and he does not create evil. So, you ask, where did evil come from? God allowed it as a possibility, as a potentiality (but not necessarily as an inevitability). God allows evil to exist as a natural consequence of choice, and true choice is a necessary condition of true free will.

Paradoxically, God allowed for free will and the possibility of evil as a mark of his love and for the reality of true love to exist in the created order. (Remember, love is not merely an emotion but it is a choice, an act of the will; as such, there can be no true love if there is no true freedom of choice.) Throughout the Bible, love and goodness are linked to obedience to God's moral law, and hatred and evil are linked to willful disobedience to God's moral law. Now, does it make any sense to allow for a choice between obedience and disobedience to be made but then not create the scenario in which the choice is made real? That is, why create merely a hypothetical or a purely theoretical choice? This is not real choice. So, yes, God did create the garden and everything in it, and he established the parameters of good living (moral law). One of the parameters was that Adam and Eve were not to eat from that one tree, the tree of the knowledge of good and evil. God clearly said that if they eat of that tree, they would surely die (that is, physical death would enter into creation and there would be spiritual separation from God). God was not "testing" them in the sense of purposely trying to trip them up or maniacally test their resolve. This created order was no cruel test or trickery. Rather, it was a true reality with the true possibility for moral choice. Again, without the reality of choice, then we would not be free people.

Remember, it was Satan who caused the first doubt. He twisted God's word and caused confusion and doubt in human moral consciousness. In Genesis 3:4, he implanted the questioning doubt: surely God didn't say you would die, did he? Then Satan went on to deceive them into thinking that God is cruel and selfish for denying them this fruit because, according to Satan, the great deceiver, this fruit would make man like God. He convinced them that God didn't want them to progress to become gods, and he encouraged them to desire to be as God. Note, this was Satan's own sin—he was not content to be the most glorious of God's angels. Rather, he wanted to be God and to be worshiped as God. This is the root of the sin of pride, the sin of desiring to recreate God in our own image and thus to become God ourselves. So, Adam and Eve ate of the fruit, thus disobeying the moral law and rejecting God. Thus was hatred and evil introduced into the created order. We can now understand evil as disobeying the moral law and willingly acting contrary to the moral good as determined by God, the definer of good.

Note that Satan caused Adam and Eve to shift their attention away from *all* that they *did* have in the garden and to focus on the *one* thing that they were denied. Don't we do that ourselves? Don't we concentrate sometimes on the don'ts and think they are somehow more desirable than the do's? This is the nature of temptation that leads to sin. Temptation is *not* sin. We are often tempted. It's when we submit to the temptation that we sin. And, this submission to temptation begins in our hearts and minds (as Christ taught in the Sermon on the Mount—see, for example, the Gospel of Matthew, chapter 5).

This begs the next question: Why the prohibition to begin with? Many think God has these don'ts because he is an oppressive tyrant. No. He has designed us and he knows what it takes to live the perfect life of true fulfillment. As designer, he knows how we are designed, what we were designed to do, and what will hurt our design. The prohibitions are for our safety so that we will live full and joyful lives. That which violates the original design is what hurts us and causes pain and suffering. Therefore, the prohibitions are to help keep us from hurting ourselves. Note, too, that with all prohibitions, there are corresponding allowances or approved actions. Basically the opposite of a prohibition is the affirmative command; when we are told not to do something (do not murder) we are implicitly told to do the opposite (foster life). In our pride, we often grumble at the prohibitions and thus ignore the affirmations or promises linked to the prohibitions. If we were to rejoice in the affirmations, I think we'd treat the prohibitions quite differently . . . don't you?

Why, then, is there this original sin? Some people are upset that we are somehow being punished for the sin of Adam and Eve and that this condition is not fair. *Au contraire*. We are rightly and justly punished for our own sins and actions, not the sin of Adam and Eve. However, there is "original sin" or "total depravity" in the sense that as eventual children of Adam and Eve, we are born with sin nature or with evil in us. How can this be? Think about it. Why did God not want Adam and Eve to eat from the tree of the knowledge of good and evil? Because he knew that as a perfectly and infinitely good being, God himself can know and comprehend evil without being evil. But we, as finite beings with the capacity for good and evil, cannot know evil without being evil. You see the difference? So, the only way for Adam and Eve to ever have knowledge of good and evil is if they were in essence good and evil. They were created good. (Throughout the act of creation outlined in Genesis, God looked at his creation and said it was good; thus, we can conclude that they were created good.) But, they were created with the capacity to know evil by doing evil and thus become evil in the process. By rejecting God and violating the moral law, they thus knew evil. But, by knowing evil, they then became evil. Thus, they have good and evil in them; they are capable of both good and evil. Their offspring are thus begotten of them, not created originally from scratch as Adam and Eve were.

Now, this is not to say that we are not created by God in his image. We indeed are, for Scripture tells us that God knits us in our mother's womb (Psalm 139:13–16), meaning he has a direct hand in conception and the design of procreation and life. He created the genetic mechanisms by which a man and a woman procreate. But we are begotten of fallen humans (our parents) and as such, we necessarily have the attributes of fallen humans. In this respect, sin or evil in humans is genetic. That is what is meant by original sin or total depravity. We cannot ever escape evil on our own, for we already know evil as part of our very being. For humans, to know evil is to be evil, and since we all know evil, we are evil in our being. As evil beings, we thus have no right on our own to be in the presence of a purely good, holy, and righteous God. Thus, through our sin nature and our sin behavior that necessarily results from our inherited sin nature, we are necessarily cut off from the presence of God.

God in his love does not desire us to be separate from him. Yet, in his righteousness, he is also a just God, demanding justice be served against evil. How are his love and justice reconciled? Through Christ. The only way to overcome this evil that necessarily separates us from God, to have the broken relationship with God reconciled or healed, and finally to be in the presence of a holy and righteous God is through faith in Jesus Christ, who, mysteriously, is fully man and fully God and who is the only human to have lived a perfect and sinless life. In other words, Christian theism teaches that by faith in Christ, the righteousness (purity and goodness) of Christ is placed upon those who believe in him, such that when a believer stands before God, he sees his son in the believer covering his/her sin instead of seeing the person full of sin. That is why, according to the very teachings of Christ, it is necessary to believe in Christ and to accept him into your heart as Lord and Savior and to submit to him. If we do so, when we stand before God, God will see us justified through Christ. He sees Christ in us instead of merely us.

I know that's a lot to take in. Read it over, think about it, and let me know what you think.

Cheers,
Prof. Dave

Dear Prof,

Yikes, that was heavy. Yet, this explanation helps me understand a bit more why Christians focus so much on salvation through Christ alone. But, I can't help but play devil's advocate (ha ha). If we cut through all the philosophy and theology here, isn't God still just a big tester? Doesn't the act of giving someone a moral dilemma with two possible choices of action, both with eternal consequences, simply constitute the mother of all tests?!? It seems to me the distinction between "test" and "actual free will" is simply a matter of semantics. Also, it occurs to me, wasn't it all Eve's fault? Adam was just an innocent bystander.

Sincerely,
Seeker

Dear Seeker,

Well, I wouldn't push the issue of who was more responsible, the man or the woman, because the man really comes out looking rather pathetic. Think about it for a moment: it took a supremely cunning and supernaturally powerful evil figure like Satan to tempt Eve into sin, yet it took merely a fallen human to tempt Adam into sin. Then, when God asked Adam what happened, do you know what Adam did? He passed the buck, blaming Eve, and then implicated God (Genesis 3:12)! He basically said, "This woman you gave me made me do it." How lame is that?!? So, who is the weaker in constitution?

The real problem in your thoughtful devil's advocacy (literally and figuratively, if you think about it) is in the presupposition of the question or scenario itself, which is rooted in a fundamental misunderstanding of the true nature of God. In other words, the phrasing of the question itself hinges upon a certain view of God that is biblically incorrect. The problem here is that you are constructing God as a task master, as a supreme tester of wills. This is not what he is doing. He did not set up our universe for the purpose of forcing us to face a moral dilemma. Rather, he created a world in which we could experience the fullness of being, the fullness of experience that involves experiencing him. Such an experience includes true love, and this reality requires or necessitates free will, and free will cannot be real if it is not enacted, and it cannot be truly enacted unless there is the opportunity for moral choice. He created the best of possible realities that includes each of these aspects of fullness, of totality of experience. This totality of experience necessitates moral choice. It is not a test in the sense you are viewing the word *test*. He did not plunk them down in the middle of a moral dilemma and then say, ruthlessly, make your choice. (If you are a fan of Andrew Lloyd Webber's *The Phantom of the Opera*, that is what the Phantom does to Christine when he captures Raoul, strings him up, and then makes her choose either the Phantom, and Raoul lives, or Raoul, and Raoul dies. Now *that* is cruel and ruthless and no real choice at all.) Rather, God created a whole universe that includes the physical and the spiritual, and the spiritual includes free will, volition, mind, emotion, and love. So, it wasn't "the mother of all tests"; rather, it is the mother of all realities.

If we view God as a mere tester of wills, then, yes, it's just a matter of semantics. But the scenario in the Garden of Eden wasn't merely a test of will. It was reality that allowed for the fullest possible expression and experience of God. Now, this is not to say that God does not test his people. He certainly does. Abraham faced a huge test (God commanded him to sacrifice his son as a test of faith, and Abraham by faith obeyed and trusted in God, who was faithful and provided a substitute sacrifice in the form of a ram, and this becomes a picture and foreshadow of God providing his son, Jesus Christ, as our sacrificial substitute). And, Job faced a big test (God basically asked Job if he would still worship God if God allowed Satan to take away all that God gave him in the first place; Job's faith was sorely tested but he remained faithful to God, and God was faithful in return, restoring Job to fullness of life).

But, before you jump to conclusions about the nature of God in these examples, please read and study the biblical accounts in which these tests are described (Abraham's test in Genesis chapter 22, and Job's testing in the book of Job, which can be found in the Old Testament). You'll see that there is an ultimate purpose to such tests or trials. They are not merely a heavy-handed test of the will. Rather, they are trials in which the faith of the person of God is tested and then strengthened for a greater use in God's divine plan of salvation. It's easy to say you believe in God when things are going well. We ultimately come to know the true depths of our faith in God in how we respond to trials. Those who despair and blame God have little or no faith. They either realize this and then develop stronger faith, or they move further away from God. But, those with true faith cry out to God in the trial, they ask why, they seek answers in God, they draw closer to God, and they worship him, acknowledging that his ways are not their ways and that despite the confusion or lack of total understanding, they will still follow and worship him. (Many of the psalms of the Old Testament illustrate this dynamic.) Such faith is deepened and strengthened, and God blesses those of such faith with deeper understanding of his divine will and character, and they are enriched in indescribable ways spiritually and intellectually.

Note that even Jesus was tempted and tested by Satan. The result of this testing was a strengthened faith within Christ the man (we have to remember that Christ was both God and man—here I'm dealing with Christ the man). Ravi Zacharias, the noted Christian apologist (I've referenced several of his books in previous e-mails), makes an important observation in one of his lectures, noting that one result of these temptations was a strengthening in Jesus' faith such that he could have faith that God the Father would indeed fulfill his promise of the cross, that if he would deliver him from the hands of Satan in the desert, he would certainly do so on the cross. Christ answered Satan by saying, "It is written . . ." That is, Christ quoted the truth of Scripture to defend himself against the lies of Satan. This strengthened his faith in the word of God and the promises of God, thus building his faith to face the cross with assurance that it was God's will and that God would fulfill his promise of salvation.

God as an arbitrary, capricious puppet master is not the God of the Bible. This is not the true and living God. God allows for trials to enter into our lives for a divine purpose. During these hardships and trials, we can deny him altogether, we can clutch our puny fists and shake them defiantly in his face, or we can draw closer to him and rely upon him to strengthen us and to teach us important spiritual lessons that will ultimately be for our own good and for his own glory. But, before we can do the latter, we must believe in God and trust in his son, Jesus Christ, as our personal Lord and Savior.

Again, this is a lot of stuff to digest. Review the e-mails and think it over. Also, I highly recommend reading the books I referenced in the previous e-mail, particularly A. W. Tozer's *The Knowledge of the Holy* and J. I. Packer's *Knowing God*. If you are interested in reading more about the serious intellectual challenges and spiritual blessings of pursuing a relationship with God, consider reading Os Guinness's *The Call: Finding and Fulfilling the Central Purpose of Your Life*, and John Piper's *Desiring God*. And, for an in-depth discussion of how trials and hardship build faith and bring about ultimate spiritual blessing, see Carson's *How Long, O Lord?: Reflections on Suffering Evil*, Guinness's *Unspeakable: Facing Up to the Challenge of Evil*, and Zacharias's *Has Christianity Failed You?*

Cheers,
Prof. Dave

Exchange 17

Can You Explain Original Sin? Why Am I Responsible for Adam's Sin? And Why Was Jesus Sacrificed?

Dear Prof,

    Thanks so much for your recent response to my last question. Believe it or not, it really helped a lot. You might not think so, because I keep asking more and more questions. You are probably banging your head against the wall right now. I need to ask yet another question. I really have been thinking long and hard about these issues, trying to make sense of them. What has really been bothering me lately is that I *still* don't fully understand the whole sacrifice-for-man's-sins thing. I mean, I kind of understand it but not as well as I would like to. I still have a lot of problems with this for some reason. How is it that all of man has to suffer because of Adam—one person? For example, if one person in a company steals, would it be right for everyone who works there or whoever works there afterward to get fired? It seems unreasonable for *all* of mankind, forever, to have to bear the burden of one person's mistake. And it was God who decided this, so why can't he just get rid of the burden? I know he has to show justice, which is good, but he is the one who put the burden on everyone rather than the *one* person who sinned. Basically, why am I responsible for Adam's sin? And there is still the sacrifice issue. Why does someone, or something, have to *die* to make God happy, or to atone for something? That seems kind of weird. To kill something doesn't seem very nice or godly. To kill a person, Jesus, in order to atone for something or to appease God seems even harsher and more tyrannical.

Sincerely,
Seeker

Dear Seeker,

You are very welcome! Again, it is my honor and my privilege to discuss these matters with you. It is also my duty as a Bible-believing follower of Christ. Jesus instructed his followers to discuss these truths with others, and it is truly a joy to have this opportunity to answer your questions. You have asked yet another *huge* question that theologians still discuss and debate. The doctrine of original sin or the depravity of humanity is the most denied doctrine today. People generally do not like to think of themselves or humans as sinful. Yet, humanity's sinful nature and clear propensity for evil is consistently confirmed by history and everyday events. We can deny sin all we want, but we cannot refute the evidence of its existence.

The confusion about original sin comes from a misunderstanding of what that doctrine is really saying. This confusion, I think, comes from a lack of clarity from church teachings, but also from the way many skeptics and atheists misconstrue the doctrine of original sin as a rhetorical tactic, to prove Christianity is a hateful, antihuman religion. Secular humanists and atheists want desperately to believe in the innate goodness of man. But this is a long-lost idealistic dream of Rousseau and the Enlightenment. (Actually, it goes back much earlier than that; for example, the ancient Chinese philosopher Confucius from around the sixth century BC believed that the individual is inherently good and that society makes people bad.) A quick empirical example: children who can't even talk yet do not by nature share their toys. Children by nature are selfish, not giving. They have to be taught to share. Similarly, very young children do not have to be taught to lie or to be deceitful. If humanism were true (that man is innately good), then children should naturally share and naturally tell the truth. But the reality is that they simply do not do these good things on their own or by nature. It is clear that humans must be taught how to be morally good; by nature, we gravitate toward evil.

This is where the doctrine of original sin or total depravity comes into play. Note that the Bible and this doctrine of original sin *do not* teach that we are all paying for the sins of Adam, that we are somehow unfairly penalized for the sins of another. This is a powerful misconception. We are not held accountable for the sins of Adam. God rightly judges us for our own sins. I think a helpful principle in understanding the sinful nature of humanity is the notion that like begets like. The idea of begetting is different from creating. When we or God create, something other than the self is created. That is why theism differs from pantheism. Theism holds that God created the universe out of nothing; God created something that is separate and different than himself. Pantheists, on the other hand, believe that the universe is God, that all of creation or reality is identical with God. However, we must understand that creating means constructing or fashioning something separate from and different in nature than the self. For example, God is eternal while the universe is not; therefore, the universe is different and separate from God. Thus, theism holds that God created the universe and it is not identical to God.

Begetting means to create from the self, to produce something that is similar in nature to the self. So, when humans have children, they are not *creating* children; rather, they are *begetting* them. Thus, the children are alike in kind and nature to the parents. Similarly, Jesus, as the only begotten Son of God, is alike in nature to God—divine and sinless. Jesus (the man) was born (begotten) of the Virgin Mary and thus has the human nature (Jesus as man), but Jesus (God) is *begotten* of God and thus is also divine in nature. (In the Christian doctrine of the Trinity, we understand that God is three divine persons in one eternal nature, and Jesus, the second person of the Trinity, is two natures—fully man and fully God—in one person. It may be helpful for us to discuss the Trinity at a later time.)

What does all this have to do with the question of original sin? God created Adam and Eve without sin but with the potential to sin (recall our previous discussion of the nature of reality that God created, a universe with free will). As we've discussed, free will is the foundational cornerstone to God's creation. (Please note, theologians and philosophers continue to discuss this complex notion of human free will, and what I present here is based upon what I believe to be a most reasonable and scriptural understanding of human free will. If you want to go into much more detail on the complexities of the Christian views of free will, then I recommend reading and comparing R. C. Sproul's *Chosen by God* and Norman Giesler's *Chosen but Free*.)

Without free will there is no true love (remember, love is not merely a feeling but a choice to commit to the good of another regardless of your own self-interest), and true love is what God wanted his creation to experience. When Adam sinned (through a free choice to disobey God), he then became a sinful being. Sin was then part of his very nature (review my previous e-mail). As a limited being, he could not know sin without being sinful. Humans are unlike the infinitely good God who can know sin without being sinful. This was the ultimate deception of Satan to Adam and Eve. Satan said that if they eat from the tree of the knowledge of good and evil, they would become as gods, knowing good and evil and thus be true moral beings like a god (Genesis chapter 3). What he didn't tell them was that the only way for them to know evil is to be evil, to take evil upon themselves as part of their nature. When they disobeyed God and ate of that fruit, they added evil onto their originally good nature (the evil was to transgress against God's law—there was nothing mystical or magical about the fruit that made them evil). So, when Adam and Eve sinned, they became evil. There is much debate in Christian theology about sin nature. For our purposes here, let's just realize that after Adam and Eve sinned, their natures became sinful (their nature was "full of sin").

Here is where the creating/begetting distinction becomes important. As sinful beings, Adam and Eve begot children who were like them in nature. The offspring of Adam and Eve were also sinful. We are not born good or innocent. We are born "in sin." This is what King David means in Psalm 51:5 when he writes, "Behold, I was brought forth in iniquity, and in sin did my mother conceived me." This phrase does *not* mean that sex is the sin that makes us sinful. Sex as designed and ordained by God is beautiful. By design, sex is to occur between a committed, married man and woman for the purposes of procreation and forming a deep intimate bond between the parents so as to create the ideal environment in which to raise children. Like anything else, sinful humans can take a beautiful thing and pervert it. Born "in sin" simply means we are born with a sinful nature, because our parents are sinful by nature. This sin nature goes back to the original parents who became sinful.

Because we are born sinful, we commit sins, and our sins are conscious and willful. We willingly sin, and we must answer for those sins. Paul tells us the wages of sin is death (Romans 6:23). This statement reveals the simple truth that God is pure, holy, and just. He will not allow sin or evil to stand in his presence. This is just and right. So, sinful creatures (us) cannot on our own merit stand in his presence. The just and fair thing is that we be forever out of his holy presence (this is death). We have no right or ability on our own to be in his holy presence. Yet his great love and desire for his creatures is that we be in his presence eternally. That is why Paul completes the thought in Romans 6:23 with this truth: "but the free gift of God is eternal life in Christ Jesus our Lord." That was God's plan from the beginning. How can he allow his sinful creatures to stand in his presence while still staying true to his holiness and justice? For justice to be served, there must be punishment for sin. Without such punishment, God is no longer just. If the punishment for sin is physical and spiritual death (to die in the body and to be spiritually out of the presence of God), then this punishment must be enacted. But upon whom? If we take this punishment ourselves, which is our due, then we die. But, if we die, then we are no longer where God wants us—in God's presence. What, then, is the solution to this dilemma?

You might be thinking that we've covered this material before. Indeed, we have, but it is vitally important that you understand these concepts. Therefore, I want to review them. God provides a substitute to take our place and to receive the just punishment in our place. Through the person of Jesus, God sacrifices himself and thus takes the punishment that is rightly ours. His justice is served and his love expressed. Through Christ's death on the cross, God sacrificed himself, so that we would not have to experience this proper punishment, which is our due. Why Christ? (And here, the Trinity again comes into play.) To stand in for sinful humans, the sacrifice must be human. Thus Jesus has the human nature. To atone for the sins of other humans, the sacrifice must be sinless. If the sacrifice is sinful, then he dies only for himself and not others. So, to die for others the sacrifice must be pure and sinless. Jesus was a man who was tempted of Satan as we are but who resisted temptation and remained sinless. Therefore, he can die for us. But if this sacrifice is to die for *all* who believe in Christ, then he must be more than mere man. At best, a sinless mere man could only die for one other human. Therefore, the sacrifice must also be "large" enough to atone for all who believe in him. Thus, Jesus is also divine; that is, infinite in nature. Only Jesus as God is "big enough" to die for all who believe in Christ, even for the sins of the whole world (1 John 2:2).

The Bible also makes clear that Christ's self-sacrifice that was "once and for all" is not automatically applied to all people. He died once, thus no more need for any other sacrifices (the Old Testament sacrificial system was in anticipation of Christ's final atoning sacrifice, which put an end to the need for these sacrifices), and he died for all, meaning his act can be applied to all people. But, it is not automatically applied to all people; rather, it is applied to all who believe in Christ. (John 3:16 says, "For God so loved the world, that he gave his only Son, that whoever believes in him should not perish but have eternal life.") Jesus himself said, "I am the way, and the truth, and the life. No one comes to the Father except through me" (John 14:6). In other words, only those who believe in Jesus can have access to God or be in his presence for eternity. Jesus also said, "Truly, truly, I say to you, unless one is born again he cannot see the kingdom of God" (John 3:3). To be "born again" simply means renewed in spirit from above or from heaven. We are "born again" only by faith in Jesus, by believing in him as our Savior.

Basically, we need to accept his claims as true and believe that he is who he claimed to be (God), believe that he was a real historical person, believe that he was both a sinless man and fully God, believe that he died on the cross for our sins, believe that he was raised from the dead in triumph over death and sin, and believe that he will come again to usher in God's kingdom and establish the new heaven and earth. We must understand and believe that we are a sinful people in need of salvation, confess our sins (that is, agree with God that he is pure and we are not and admit that we are sinful), accept this gift of Christ knowing in our heart and mind that if we believe all these things as really true that we will be saved from the punishment that is duly ours, and then sincerely repent of our sins.

The word *repent* means to turn away or to turn around. The idea behind repenting is to turn 180 degrees away from sin. If you accept Christ into your heart (believe all these things are true), then Christ taught that you will be saved from eternal death. (John 3:16: "For God so loved the world, that he gave his only Son, that whoever believes in him should not perish but have eternal life.")

Faith in Christ not only affords us salvation, but it also changes us for the better. We are recreated spiritually. When we truly accept Christ as savior, we become a new creation, a new person, and we will desire the good and will turn away from sin and evil (2 Corinthians 5:17; Ephesians 4:17–24; 1 John 2:5–6). This is called sanctification—the process of becoming sanctified, or set apart, as a child of God. This process is lifelong. After you accept Christ, your desire will be to pursue virtue as revealed by God. But, you are still a human being with a sin nature. You will be tempted, and you may sin. But God forgives you if you sincerely and honestly confess the sin to God and ask for his strength and guidance to resist that sin in the future (you can pray directly to God and confess to him directly; see 1 John 1:9). If you truly accept Christ, you will see a change in your thinking, in your desires, in your behavior, in your speech. It isn't just that you are blindly following a list of do's and don'ts. No—it is because God has given you a new mind and spirit and you have a new desire to please him and to follow him, knowing and believing that as our Creator, he knows what is best for us.

Then when you stand before God on Judgment Day, you will be judged, but you will *not* be condemned. What a glorious promise, what a joyous truth! When you accept Christ into your heart and believe all these things, God will look at you on Judgment Day and he will not see your sinful self. Instead, he will see the righteousness of Christ. Christ's sinless nature is imputed to you (that is, attributed or ascribed to you). Your sin nature is covered by Christ's pure nature, and God accepts you because you accepted Christ. Then, the Bible teaches, in the last days, all the believers will be recreated and be given pure bodies, pure minds, pure spirits, and we will live for eternity in a recreated heaven and earth in the presence of an infinitely pure, loving, wise, just, and holy God (see 1 Corinthians 15: 51–57; Philippians 3:20–21; and Revelation chapter 21). This will *not* be a dull existence, for God is infinite and eternal, and we will spend an eternity always in the process of knowing and experiencing the infinite.

I hope this helps a bit. This is serious business, and I want you to be sure of your knowledge, not just your knowledge of this material but of the knowledge of your eternal destiny. The question is simply this: What will be your eternal destiny? I want you to be sure of the answer and to understand why your answer is true, whatever it happens to be. Everyone has an answer to that question, but is the answer *true*? I want you to be sure your answer is true.

Cheers,
Prof. Dave

Exchange 18

What's the Deal with the Trinity? It Seems Like a Total Contradiction to Me.

Dear Prof,

Some issues are starting to gel for me in my mind, but your explanation of God's self-sacrifice on the cross through Jesus lost me a bit when you mentioned the Trinity. I just don't get this Trinity business. In a course on basic logic, I learned about contradictions, and it seems to me that the Christian notion of three divine persons in one is a total contradiction, plain and simple. And, it seems to smack of polytheism—is the Christian God three gods or one? Also, I've heard that the Trinity is totally made up, that it isn't even in the Bible, and that it was added much later. Help me out here, please, because I'm totally confused.

Sincerely,
Seeker

Dear Seeker,

When I was writing my previous response, I knew that this would be your next question. How could it not be? Please note that the doctrine of the Trinity is not an easy topic to understand. There is much confusion and misinformation about this doctrine, both outside and inside the Christian community. I will do my best to explain my understanding of it to you, as briefly and succinctly as I can. If you are still having questions about it, we may want to discuss it over a coffee (or two or three) in person, because I may be able to address some of your deeper questions more readily in a face-to-face conversation. Here goes . . .

By way of introduction, let's outline a few key concepts. The doctrine of the Trinity is an essential doctrine for orthodox, biblical Christianity, and this doctrine is fully biblical and is part of the earliest teachings of Christianity. Contrary to the claims made by the popular press, fictional books like *The Da Vinci Code*, and popular scholars (popular in the media but who are challenged and refuted by leading, serious biblical scholars), the Trinity was not made up at the time of the Council of Nicea in 325 AD. Interestingly, there are quotes from early church leaders and fathers as far back as the first century AD in which the Trinity is specifically mentioned; therefore, it doesn't make sense to claim or to conclude that this doctrine was made up and added to Christian belief in the fourth century AD.

What happened was basically this: not until the fourth century when major heresies (teachings that contradicted the teachings of the New Testament) started to develop do we see more explicit councils, like the Council of Nicea, articulating the doctrine of the Trinity. It is important to understand that over the centuries, the church called different councils in order to clarify scriptural truth and to refute heresies and false teachings that were cropping up. This is not unusual. Remember, a main reason the Gospels of the New Testament were written in the first century (only a few decades after Christ) was to set down clearly the teachings of Christ. The various letters in the New Testament were written, among other reasons, in order to correct false teachings that were popping up from teachers who were not disciples of Jesus and who were making things up on their own. In order for early believers to distinguish true teachings from false teachings, Jesus' disciples wrote the various documents that later became known as the New Testament. Throughout these writings, the concept of the Trinity is present. However, as time went on, later thinkers misunderstood the truth or mixed some of the truth with other ideas (like some Hebrew legal teachings, Jewish mythology, and Greek philosophical concepts) and started to teach contrary ideas about the nature and person of Jesus that contradicted the clear teachings of New Testament Scripture. Thus, by the fourth century, a council was called to clarify the doctrine of the Trinity.

The doctrine of the Trinity is basically the fullest expression of our limited understanding of God's divine nature. Trinity simply means triunity or triune—threeness in one: there is ultimate plurality in unity, or diversity in unity. In other words, eternally present in the First-Cause (God), there is always already both plurality or diversity as well as unity (the ultimate expression of unity in diversity). God is not a simple unity; rather, he is three divine persons in one divine being or nature; another way to think of this is: three whos in one what or three personalities in one essence. God is singular in nature (monotheistic) but is expressed or manifest as three persons. Yet, these persons are not separate entities (that would be polytheism); rather, they are eternally and continually a single nature. This is not a logical contradiction. It is not saying that God is three persons in one person or three natures in one nature. These constructions would be logical contradictions. However, the Trinity distinguishes between the category *person* and the category *nature*. Thus, to say that God is three persons in one nature is not a logical contradiction, because of the categorical difference between *person* and *nature*. It is a difficult concept to fully understand, but it is not a contradiction. As such, it takes special revelation (the word of God) to understand the Trinity. It is so unique and complex that our finite minds cannot conceive of it on our own, nor can we derive this from natural theology (an understanding of God derived from observing the created universe). This truth about God's nature is known only through his self-revelation in Scripture.

So, how does the Bible reveal this triune nature of God? It is true that the theological term *Trinity* does not itself appear in the Bible. However, the whole counsel of the word of God clearly teaches the two main concepts of the Trinity: (1) there is but one God, and he is one (monotheism); and (2) there are three distinct persons: God the Father, God the Son, and God the Holy Spirit. Here are a few examples of Scripture that teach God is one. In Exodus chapter 20 (in the Old Testament) where God reveals the Ten Commandments to Moses, we see that whole discourse rooted in the theological premise that God is one (monotheism). In Deuteronomy 6:4 (also the Old Testament) we see an explicit proclamation that Judaism is monotheistic, thus unique and distinct from the other polytheistic Near Eastern religions. In Mark 12:28–31 (the New Testament), where Jesus is discussing the Law or the Ten Commandments, he begins by affirming the oneness of God (just as God did when he revealed the Commandments to Moses). Note, that even as Jesus affirms the oneness of God here, in Mark 12:36 he asserts the plurality of divine persons. Here's a last example: in his letter to the Christian believers in Corinth, Paul addresses their question about eating food offered to pagan idols, and he starts his answer by affirming the oneness of God, that God is one, not many (1 Corinthians 8:4–6). So, the first point here is that the Trinity is grounded in monotheism. The triune God is Three in One, not three different gods.

The second main point is that the Bible reveals God to be unity in diversity, to have multiple (namely three) persons in one divine nature, and this truth is expressed throughout the Bible, from the very beginning (Genesis in the Old Testament) to the very end (Revelation in the New Testament). To be clear, though, the Trinity as such is not explicitly taught in the Old Testament; however, the plurality of persons within the Godhead is clearly expressed in the Old Testament. Take the very first line of the Bible found in Genesis 1:1: "In the beginning, God created the heavens and the earth." In the original Hebrew, the plural form for God (*elohim*) is used here, not the singular (*el*) or the singular poetic (*eloah*); yet, the singular form of the verb to create is used here. Similarly in Genesis 1:26 we read, "Then God [singular] said [plural], 'Let us make [plural] man in our [plural] image.'" Why did Moses use this Hebrew grammar and sentence structure? Some suggest that he used the plural form to indicate the royal majesty of God. However, such usage was not common to Hebrew or other Near Eastern cultures in the fifteenth century BC. Their kings were referred to in the singular, and in the Bible the various kings are grammatically referred to in the singular. Therefore, many Christian commentators agree that this usage (plural *elohim* with singular verb) indicates a uniplurality within the Godhead, that is, a singular essence with a plurality of powers or personhood.

In the New Testament, we see through the teachings and experiences of Christ that this uniplurality within the Godhead is specifically trinitarian (three persons in one nature), namely God the Father, God the Son, and God the Holy Spirit. There are many passages throughout the New Testament to illustrate this; here are a few from the Gospel of Matthew. In Matthew 3:16–17, we see Christ the Son being baptized, the Holy Spirit descending, and the Father speaking, proclaiming Christ as the Son in the presence of the Holy Spirit. And, in Matthew 28:17–20, Jesus gives what is called the Great Commission, and he does so in the name of the Father, the Son, and the Holy Spirit (the full expression of God's name and nature). In this episode, we also see the evidence that the disciples understood Christ to be God (the Son), because they explicitly worshiped him as only God should be worshiped, Christ is given all authority as only God should have, his commandments are equivalent to God's for he is God, and he is eternally present as only God can be. The consistent revelation throughout the Bible is that God is a uniplurality, and specifically, he is triune. Therefore, we have the doctrine of the Trinity that provides the theological explanation of God's triune nature.

There are some noted challenges to this doctrine of the Trinity:

1. It is illogical or a contradiction. We've already discussed that this is not a violation of the law of noncontradiction; it is a mystery but not a contradiction. It may go against the reason's ability to comprehend completely, but it does not violate reason's ability to apprehend consistently. Remember, the doctrine distinguishes between the category of *person* and *nature*; thus, to claim God is three persons in one nature is not a contradiction. To say he is three persons in one person or three natures in one nature would be.

2. It is polytheism. As outlined above, this doctrine is not polytheistic but explicitly monotheistic. There is oneness of essence (monotheism) and plurality of persons. God is not three separate essences. God is one being with three persons, one what and three whos. Again, this is a mystery but not a contradiction, and it totally asserts the oneness of God or monotheism. Unity or oneness does not necessarily require or mean singularity. In Qur'anic Islam, Allah has singularity and unity, but in biblical Christianity God has unity and plurality (for this and many other reasons, Allah of the Qur'an and the God of the Bible are not the same).

3. Christ is not God and thus cannot be a person in the Trinity (an objection offered by Muslims, Jehovah's Witnesses, and Mormons). We have already discussed the evidence of Christ's divinity in earlier e-mails: Christ claimed to be Yahweh, to be identical with God the Father, to be "I Am"; Christ claimed the glory of God; Christ accepted worship from man as only God should; Jesus forgave sins and raised the dead under his own authority as only God can; and his disciples attributed deity to him throughout their ministry and teaching. The doctrine of the Trinity best explains the truth and reality of Christ's divinity.

4. Christ as God and man is a contradiction. This claim that Christ is fully man and fully God is no less a contradiction than the Trinity itself (note that the principle of Christ as fully God and fully man is part and parcel of the doctrine of the Trinity). The doctrine is not saying that Christ is God and not-God or man and not-man. This would

be a contradiction. Rather, the doctrine states that God is three whos in one what; and Jesus is two whats in one who; that is, Jesus has two natures (God and man) in one person (God the Son).

So, that's the doctrine of the Trinity in a nutshell. But, before I close this lengthy email, I want to discuss some reasons as to why this doctrine is so important. What theological and spiritual significance does it hold? Here are a few answers to that question:

1. Unity in diversity in the first cause. Ravi Zacharias (the noted Christian apologist I frequently reference) makes this point quite powerfully in many of his lectures. Throughout human intellectual and cultural history there is a pursuit to achieve unity in diversity. The achievement of this goal is only possible because it was always already achieved in God in the first cause—the Trinity is the accomplishment of unity in diversity in the absolute. Because there is unity in diversity in the first cause (triune God as causal agent of reality as we know and experience it), there is the hope of achieving it in the effect (that is, in the reality that he created for us to experience). Specifically, there is hope in Christ that humanity can achieve true unity in diversity. Note that this unity is not an annihilation of self but a celebration of self in relationship or in community with God and others who are God's children through Christ.

2. True community in the first cause. Unity in diversity is achieved through true community. Community is part of the first cause (the Godhead—Father, Son, and Holy Spirit—is a community of persons in a singular divine nature) and is the ideal state of reality. Community with God and with each other is broken by human sin, but through Christ we can regain community with the Godhead and thus with each other. Christ is the only answer for racism and all other sin and social ills that separate humans from each other. Our sin first separates us from God, and we achieve forgiveness and reunion with God by faith through Christ, and by faith we then receive a changed heart and attitude that allows us to heal the separations and broken relationships in our human existence. The Christian practice of communion (or the Lord's Supper) is the expression of that restored community, that in Christ we are bound to God and to each other in a perfect union.

3. True love in the first cause—source of all meaning, morality, purpose, destiny. True love requires one who loves, one who is loved, and the spirit of love. This is seen only in the Trinity (Father, Son, and Holy Spirit). Because true love exists in the first cause, we can experience it in the effect, in our lives. Because God is personal and is love, we can have a personal relationship with him through Christ. And, because of this personal relationship with God through Christ, we can repair our earthly relationships and have real love in our lives.

I know that's a lot of information, and I don't expect you to get it all in one gulp. There are many Christian believers who struggle to understand the Trinity, but they do believe based on faith. However, I hope that my response demonstrates that there are good reasons supporting such faith, that it is not mere blind faith. In other words, I hope I've showed you that there is much content, fact, philosophy, history, and theology to support this Christian belief in the doctrine of the Trinity. If you want to read further, see the following:

Lewis, C. S. *Mere Christianity*. New York: HarperCollins, 1952.

Geisler, Norman. "Trinity." *Baker Encyclopedia of Christian Apologetics*. Grand Rapids: Baker, 1999. 730–37.

Geisler, Norman, and Frank Turek. *I Don't Have Enough Faith to Be an Atheist*. Wheaton, IL: Crossway, 2004.

Packer, J. I. *Knowing God*. Downers Grove, IL: InterVarsity, 1993.

Sproul, R. C. *Essential Truths of the Christian Faith*. Carol Stream, IL: Tyndale House, 1993.

Tozer, A. W. *The Knowledge of the Holy: The Attributes of God*. New York: HarperCollins, 1978.

Zacharias, Ravi, and Norman Geisler, eds. *Who Made God? And Answers to over 100 Other Tough Questions of Faith*. Grand Rapids: Zondervan, 2003.

Cheers,
Prof. Dave

EXCHANGE 19

Why Did Christ Have to Die?

Dear Prof,

Thank you for that detailed explanation of the Trinity. I can't say that I fully understand it, but I feel more confident in knowing that it just isn't made up out of thin air. There is much more history, philosophy, and theology behind it than I ever expected. But, I'm still having serious questions about the death of Christ. This just seems so horrific and barbaric to me. I keep wondering, was that really necessary? I know you discussed why Christ died on the cross a few e-mails ago, but I'm still not sure I understand. Can you go over that again? Thanks.

Sincerely,
Seeker

Dear Seeker,

I am more than happy to discuss this question again, because it really is the very heart of Christianity. Without Christ and the cross, there is no true Christianity. And, I agree, it *is* gruesome and barbaric, because humanity in its sin is by nature gruesome and barbaric. It is a messy ordeal, but God resolved it all in that one historic moment. From the midst of the gruesome barbarity exercised against the pure and sinless Christ at the hands of evil, sinful men, God brought forth the greatest possible good: the fulfillment of his divine promise to provide salvation from the penalty of sin (eternal death or separation from God) and to restore relationship with his beloved creatures. All those who, by faith, believe in the Son will know the Father and be reunited with God. (Throughout this discussion, I will be referring to the different Persons of God, and I will be distinguishing between Jesus the man and Jesus as God, so you may want to review the e-mail on the Trinity if you get confused.) I will do my best to explain why it was necessary for Christ to die the way he did.

There are a few important presuppositional truths that we must first review and clearly understand about the nature of God and the nature of humanity. (We have discussed this before, but it is helpful to put it all together in this one section.) God is necessarily pure, good, holy, righteous, just, fair, and loving. Humanity, after its fall into sin, is by nature impure, evil, unholy, unrighteous, unfair, and unloving. God made humans to be free moral agents who were originally unfallen and pure. Adam and Eve were created sinless, but they had free will and were free moral agents. By choice they could be morally good and do that which one ought to do; that is, to follow the moral law of God, which is the standard by which we know good and evil. God was open and clear about the moral law, making it plainly known to Adam and Eve. Satan deceived Eve (who then deceived Adam) and planted the seed of pride, and as a result Adam and Eve both chose to disobey God's command not to eat from the tree of the knowledge of good and evil. In their disobedience, Adam and Eve came to know evil by experience and thus became evil in nature. God is purely good and omniscient, and he can know evil without doing or being evil. Humans are not omniscient, and they came to know or understand evil by doing and thus becoming evil.

Evil by definition is rejecting or working contrary to that which is good; evil is a privation of good; evil is transgressing what ought to be; evil is attempting to replace the absolute definition of good with one's own subjective definition and thus attempting to subvert the absolute good. God's basic moral command is to obey him. This is not a self-serving or egotistical command. God in his perfection is worthy of love and obedience, and since God is purely good his commands are purely good. To obey him is to thus be good. To disobey that which is purely good is by definition evil. When humans disobeyed God, by experience they knew evil. However, the only way for a human to know evil is also to be evil. Once humans disobeyed God, they were by nature evil. This is original sin (review the e-mail on original sin).

As hard as it may be to accept, there is a necessary privation of good in us. We are no longer purely good. This is undeniable. Look around at how humans have acted throughout history, look at how people you know act, look inside your own heart, look at your own actions and thoughts. Humanism and some Eastern philosophies teach that humans are innately good. But just look at the behavior of infants, for example. You don't have to teach children to lie, cheat, or to be selfish. They do so naturally. But, you do have to teach them how to be good. Like it or not, humans are by nature evil. We are self-motivated to rally against the good, to disobey the precepts of a holy and good God. Because of our sin nature or the evil that is clearly in us, we cannot be in the presence of a holy and purely good God. We have no right or ability on our own merits. Our natures necessarily separate us eternally from God. That is the crisis of the human condition. This is the result of our sin. Thus, Paul writes in his letter to the Romans, "for all have sinned and fall short of the glory of God" (Romans 3:23).

Keeping in mind that since God is good, holy, righteous, and just, he would be perfectly just and fair in allowing us all to be eternally separated from him (what Christian theology traditionally calls hell). The separation is our own fault. The penalty of our sin is physical and spiritual death—eternal separation from a purely good God. This penalty or consequence is totally logical, fair, reasonable, and just (which are essential qualities of God). Ah, but God is also loving and merciful. His desire is for his creation to be with him for eternity (1 Tim 2:4 says that God desires all people to be saved and to come to know the truth). That is why he created us—so that we might experience his love and give him glory by worshiping him, because he is truly and exclusively worthy of worship. Again, this is not an ego trip for God. It is a simple truth that follows logically and naturally from his divine and perfect nature. He created us for his glory and for our benefit, so that we might experience the immeasurable joy of worshiping him in spirit and truth and experiencing his boundless love.

Now that we understand God's nature, our nature, and our predicament of eternal separation from God effected by our own sinful identities, essences, and behaviors, what's the answer to our predicament? How are we to be rejoined to God, regain fellowship and community with him? God must become man and take upon himself the punishment that we justly deserve so that we might be reunited with him. The sacrifice of Christ was thus necessary. Historical Christianity explains the necessity of Christ's sacrifice and the resulting salvation in terms of five key principles: propitiation, redemption, justification, reconciliation, and sanctification. These are fundamental to Christianity, and I will do my best to describe them clearly yet briefly.

1. Propitiation: This theological term means to satisfy the holy wrath or just anger of God against sin. Remember, God is purely good, and he cannot tolerate evil. Any evil act must be punished for the sake of justice, and it must be destroyed and removed from God's presence. Only then is God's proper wrath against evil assuaged. Many people are uncomfortable with and downright hostile to the notion of God's wrath. They want him to be only good and loving. However, we must understand that God would not be truly good nor loving if he did not show proper wrath against sin and evil. A truly good God cannot tolerate evil. Would it be unloving for you to have proper anger against a man who murdered your sibling? Of course not, so why should we deny God his righteous wrath against sin and evil? The only way for us to assuage his justified wrath against our sin is to die as is our just punishment for our sin. But, in God's love, he died in our place in the person of Christ. God satisfies justice and thus propitiates (assuages and satisfies) his wrath so that we don't have to experience his righteous wrath ourselves.

2. Redemption: This term means to buy back, to pay a debt, or to pay an obligation. Our debt for our sin is death (Romans 6:23). God through Christ paid that debt by dying on the cross in our place. As such, God has redeemed, or bought back, or paid the debt for those who believe. Note, too, that the fact of this redemption, bought at a very high cost by God himself, is the source of Christian love for and worship of God. How can the believer not love and desire to worship a loving, self-sacrificing God who redeemed the sinner? Redemption saves the believer from the penalty of his or her sin, and it also produces within the believer the reasonable and natural response of adoration, appreciation, and worship.

3. Justification: As noted earlier, God is righteous and just. His divinely just nature requires that justice be served. The penalty of sin is death (separation from God due to our sin), so death must be experienced for justice to be served. God the Son through Christ died a physical death and experienced the alienation from the Father that we rightly should experience because of our own sins. We know Christ experienced that alienation because it is recorded in the New Testament that he cried out on the cross, "My God, my God, why have you forsaken me?" (Matthew 27:46; Mark 15:34). Jesus as man experienced separation

from God the Father. So, Jesus took upon Himself our punishment so that we might be justified, that is, made morally and legally right in the eyes of God's justice. God is just and he is our justifier. That is, he makes us able to satisfy the expectations of his righteous law. If we accept Christ as God, believe he died for our sins, acknowledge him as our Lord and Savior, live our lives according to his will (which is perfect and exceedingly better than our own will for our lives), then when we stand before God at the final judgment, he will see the righteousness of Christ in us instead of seeing our unrighteous self. The righteousness of Christ is credited to us or imputed to us. Through faith in Christ, we are made just or justified in God's eyes.

4. Reconciliation: Through the sacrifice of Christ (God sacrificing himself through Christ), those who believe are then reconciled or reunited with God. Our sin separates us from God. Faith in the redemptive work of Christ reunites us with God. Through faith in Christ, we are no longer at war with God, we no longer desire to be separate from God, and we are invited to be in community with God. Our own rebellion and sin put us at war with God, but faith in Christ's work on the cross makes peace with God and reconciles us with God. Even though we declared war on God, it is God who declares peace and who fulfills the requirements of this peace treaty for us. Through faith in Christ, we are granted this peace and reconciliation.

5. Sanctification: If we truly believe in the life, death, and resurrection of Christ, our lives are necessarily changed. In his letter to the church in Ephesus, the Apostle Paul talks about shedding the old self and putting on the new self, which is fashioned after the righteousness and holiness of God (Ephesians 4:22–24). Believers in Christ are new creations and are gradually transformed into the very image of Christ. We are made in God's image, but we are sinful (because of our sinful human lineage). When we acknowledge Christ as Savior and Lord of our lives, then our hearts and minds are re-created in the image of Christ, and our lives are different. We have a new mind, new heart, new morality, new interests, and a new desire to worship God and to do his will. This process of change is called sanctification, which literally means to be set apart, to be different. It is a gradual, difficult, sometimes painful, lifelong process, and the presence of this positive change in our lives is evidence of our true faith in Christ.

Jesus died a sacrificial and atoning death on the cross and rose from the dead so as to achieve these eternal spiritual benefits for those who believe. These aspects of salvation are not automatically applied to everyone. We must individually make a conscious decision to acknowledge Christ and to believe in him as described above. Only then can we begin a relationship with God through Christ and truly know God. The Apostle John, explaining the core teachings of Christ, wrote, "Whoever who has the Son [Christ] has life; whoever does not have the Son of God does not have life" (1 John 5:12). To accept Christ and to know him in this way (and thus to know God) is what the Bible means by being "born again." This term is often misunderstood and misrepresented these days. The Greek expression (the original language of the New Testament) actually means to be born from above, to experience a spiritual rebirth. Christ said, "Truly, truly, I say to you, unless one is born again he cannot see the kingdom of God" (John 3:3). Thus, salvation is not about religion. It is about a relationship with God through Christ. No one is born a Christian. No one is a Christian merely by being raised in a Christian home, in a Christian family. No one is a Christian merely by attending a Christian church. A person is a Christian only by personally and individually acknowledging Christ as Savior and Lord. This is the teaching of Christ from the very beginning, and it has been the core teaching of historic Christianity ever since.

Why did God become man through Christ and then die? Man sinned and the penalty is death. Therefore a man must die. We can die ourselves for our sins, but that accomplishes only justice. We are still dead and separated from God. Therefore, God became human to die for humans (a divine mystery, but not a contradiction—review the e-mail on the Trinity). But, this human who dies in our place must be pure. If this human is sinful, then his death accomplishes nothing beyond justice for himself (though not salvation for himself). Therefore, the human must be pure, without sin. Jesus as God is holy and pure—sinless. Moreover, as a man, he did not sin. He was even tempted by Satan in the desert, just as Eve was tempted (and consequently, Adam as well). However, where Adam and Eve gave in to temptation and sinned, Jesus did not. He relied on the truth of Scripture rightly interpreted and applied to his life to sustain his faith, and he resisted temptation and never fell into sin. That is why it is theologically necessary and true that Christ lived a sinless life. This, too, has been the consistent teaching of historic Christianity. Christ was the only sinless human being. The sacrifice also had to be willing. It does no good to force someone to die for others. Therefore, Christ willingly accepted the task and willingly submitted to the will of the Father that he be sacrificed. The sacrifice also had to be extensive enough to atone for the sins of all the humans who believe, past, present, and future. Therefore, an infinite God sacrificed himself so that all who believe might be saved. Only God is big enough, so to speak, to atone for the sins of all who believe.

I know this is a lot, but these are key concepts that must be understood and believed. Salvation depends upon it. So, by way of review, you must have a personal faith in Christ, and you must have a personal relationship with God through Christ. Mere religion does not save. Mere good works do not save. We cannot save ourselves. Nothing we do can save ourselves from the just punishment we deserve. Remember, no matter how many good works we do, they do not erase our sin and evil deeds, and the existence of our sin nature necessarily separates us from God. We can do nothing on our own to overcome this. Only God can save us, and he does so through the life, death, and resurrection of Christ. We must have a personal relationship with Christ in order to be saved. This is why Christ said, "I am the way, and the truth, and the life. No one comes to the Father except through me" (John 14:6). There is no other way. Is this an exclusive claim? Yes, but it is one that Christ made. Christians did not make this up. Christ declared it true. (And since Christ is God and since God does not lie, this statement must be true.) It is an exclusive claim (meaning it excludes other possible ways to God), but it is *not* exclusionary. That is, this exclusive claim and promise is freely available to everyone.

As you consider this answer, you may also want to contemplate the following question: If there is more than one way to God, then why would Christ submit to this horrific death? This self-sacrificial act of God through the person of Christ does not make any sense if there are other ways to reach God. If there really are other ways to God, then there is no reason for God the Father to require that the Son submit to this atoning act. Why bother? Just let humans reach God in other ways. However, the reality that God did sacrifice himself through Christ and that Christ endured such horrific suffering in our place argues quite persuasively that it was a divinely necessary act. Thus faith in this redemptive act is the only way to be reunited with God. I realize this is an unpopular view these days, but consider the logic of the argument. It makes sense. To claim that there are other equally valid ways to reach God makes the cross of Christ completely unnecessary. Worse, it makes a mockery of the cross, suggesting that Christ was a fool for enduring this torment. No, Christ had to die for our sins, because it is the only way that we can be reunited with a holy, just, righteous, merciful, and loving God. This is the only way that all the characteristics of God can be simultaneously expressed and the only way that God could be completely consistent with the entirety of his divine nature.

I know I've already recommended *The Cross of Christ* by John Stott and *Mere Christianity* by C. S. Lewis, and if I remember correctly, you started reading them. I thought I would point out that these ideas I've discussed are analyzed more fully in both books.

Cheers,
Prof. Dave

Exchange 20

Can't I Just Understand God in My Own Way?

Dear Prof,

Hmm, I've been the one asking the questions here, and you threw me at the end of your last response with the questions you asked me to consider. I do appreciate those questions, and I understand, as you would say, the consequences of one's answers to those questions. What you say makes a lot of sense. It really does. But I have to be honest with you—I'm just not comfortable with the answers. The exclusive language . . . I don't know . . . unnerves me somehow. Also, it smacks of churchiness, and church just makes me cringe. I guess I want a belief that makes me comfortable, one that I can be happy with, one that makes me happy. I just like the view that there are many paths to God, and I want to choose my own faith system, a path that works for me. I want to integrate everything I feel passionate about and rationalized for myself, subjectively, and I am comfortable with that at this point. Anyway, won't God say I have done a pretty decent job of sifting through the mess in order to come to some kind of stable belief in him? Why can't I just try my best to reach God and to understand him in my own way? Oh, and another thought I had—why would there just be one God? Wouldn't he be lonely? Maybe that's why he created man, so he would have someone to talk to. Sorry for throwing out these seemingly random questions, but it's what I've been thinking about lately since our last exchange.

Sincerely,
Seeker

Dear Seeker,

Ah, now we are getting down to the nitty-gritty of faith and belief. You'd think that all the detailed historical, theological, and philosophical information would be the real stuff, and in many ways it all is. But, we are now moving from abstract theory to personal application, where the true challenge lies. It's one thing to intellectualize belief, yet it's quite another to internalize it. What I think you are struggling with, which everyone at some point must struggle with, is this basic question: Do I understand and accept God for who he truly is, as he has revealed himself to me, or do I choose to believe in a god I've created for myself? I pray my response helps you sort this out.

It is often said that one's religion, theology, or view of God is very personal, and I would agree with that. But the fact that one's belief is personal does not shield it from assessment and evaluation. Socrates said the unexamined life is not worth living, and so our beliefs must be examined for truthfulness and accuracy. The Bible encourages us to test our beliefs for truthfulness. Lamentations 3:40 reads, "Let us test and examine our ways, and return to the Lord." In his second letter to the church in Corinth, Paul writes, "Examine yourselves, to see whether you are in the faith. Test yourselves" (2 Corinthians 13:5). And in his first letter to the Thessalonians, Paul says, "But test everything; hold fast to what is good" (1 Thessalonians 5:21). God calls his people to reason together with him (Isaiah 1:18). Also, he promises that when we come to him with an open mind and heart, he will reveal deep and unimaginable truths: "Call to me and I will answer you, and I will tell you great and hidden things that you have not known" (Jeremiah 33:3). The infinite God of all creation encourages us to call upon him, to ask him questions, to reason with him. If nothing else, this should reinforce for you that true Christian faith is not a mere blind acceptance of dogma. Rather, it is a mindful faith that relies upon the full exercise of our intellectual, reasoning faculties.

However, what God reveals to us is an objective truth, not a subjective one. And we have to be very careful that what we believe is more than just something of our own making, or something that we feel good about, or something that is comfortable to us. Indeed, we may feel good or comfortable in the truth, but we shouldn't decide or settle upon something just because we feel good about it (or that it makes us feel good). We may feel good because something is true, but something is not true simply because we feel good about it (or because it makes us feel good). When we are looking into the nature of God, we must be sure that what we decide upon is in fact truth and not merely something that we simply feel good about or are comfortable with.

Many people today are disenchanted with the church, and this may be part of what has motivated you to seek your own path to understand God. Indeed, Christ pointed out to the Pharisees (the religious leaders in Israel during Christ's time) that they could not know God simply by keeping the law, and that deep in their hearts they did not really know God. They were putting stock in external religiosity (similar to "churchiness" as you put it) and ignoring their own heart issues (the sinful natures of their own heart and thoughts). Ultimately, the problem with the Pharisees was that they were trying to reach God their own way instead of the way God prepared for his creation.

The same problem happens today. We cannot know God simply by following rules and regulations set up by the church or by following an idea that we assemble ourselves; rather, we can only know God through the way he has established for us—through his Son, Jesus Christ. As Christ said himself, "I am the way, and the truth, and the life. No one comes to the Father except through me" (John 14:6). This is an exclusive claim, and it is either true or it isn't. If we decide it isn't true, then we must conclude that Christ was a liar and a fraud, and that his suffering, death, and resurrection were for nothing. I am convinced beyond a shadow of doubt that Christ is who he claims to be (God), that belief in him is the only way to God (as he himself says), and that the teachings of Christ as revealed in his word (the Bible) are true and trustworthy. I hope and pray that you too can come to this same level of assurance.

You state, "I want to choose my own faith system, one that works for me. I want to integrate everything I feel passionate about and rationalize it for myself, subjectively, and I am comfortable with that at this point." Notice, the emphasis in your position is on subjective expression, not objective understanding. Truth is not a subjective thing, because if it were, it would bring us back to relativism, which as we've already seen in our earlier exchanges is self-defeating and thus untrue. Also, just because something works for you doesn't make it true (this is pragmatism and it is fundamentally flawed). Something may work because it is true, but because something works doesn't make it true. So, rationalizing a belief until you are comfortable with it doesn't mean you have truth; it merely means you have an idea that you happen to like. At that point we are merely on the level of subjective taste, not objective truth. It's important to see the difference.

You ask, "Won't God say I have done a pretty decent job of sifting through the mess in order to come to some kind of stable belief in him?" You are assuming God will be pleased with your efforts, but how do you know? Are you really sure? What is the basis for this claim and conclusion? Is it because you think you've done a good enough job so God must think so too? What is the foundation for this position? According to how God has revealed himself through the only God-inspired Scripture, the Bible, he would be rather displeased with your characterization of him, because it comes from your own subjective view and not from his revelation. We have to remember that he is God, not us, and that he reveals himself and truth to us, not the other way around. Moreover, your subjective creation of him in your mind is actually an idol of your own making, not a vision of the true living God. And as such, you have actually violated one of his most fundamental moral laws, which is not to create and worship false gods.

Note that I am not being arbitrarily religious or legalistic here. I am simply applying what God has revealed to us in his word to this situation. Portions of what you think about God may in fact be true, but enough of what you think may be wrong that you move further away from God than closer to him. We must also realize that any image of God we create in our heads may be false information coming from the enemy (Satan), who is the great deceiver. Humanity's first sin was basically idolatry—believing something false about who God really is. Satan tricked Eve into thinking that God wouldn't do what he said he would do and that God was trying to trick Eve. This was false information about God, and Eve bought in to the lies. We all have to be very careful that we come to know God as he really and truly is, not as we wish or would like him to be. The only way for us truly to know him is through his Son (throughout the Gospel of John, Christ says that if we abide in the Son, who is in the Father, then we abide in the Father, and if we know the Son then we can know the Father). If we follow a god of our own making, then we will not know God and will move further and further away from him. This is not what he wants for us.

This leads us to the next logical question, which you asked: "Why would there just be one God? Wouldn't he be lonely? Maybe that's why he created man, so he would have someone to talk to." There is a lot to unpack here, but I'll do my best to keep it as brief as possible. There can only be one God. By definition, God is absolute and eternal, the infinite, uncreated first cause (review our earlier exchanges on the nature of God and basic first principles). You cannot have multiple infinite beings. Infinite is infinite, and there can only be one infinite. If you try to set up, let's say, two infinite beings, we run into the basic problem of distinguishing one from the other. Since there would be two beings, one has to be different from the other, which means one lacks something the other has (this is the most basic definition of difference—one thing is different than another because it lacks something the other has; it is the lack that makes it different). If we say one of these infinite beings lacks something the other one has, then the one that lacks something cannot be truly infinite, because an infinite being cannot lack anything (that contradicts the very definitional nature of infinite). So, there can only be one God, and this is precisely what the Bible teaches.

From this simple point, polytheism can be rejected as false (plus, given the overwhelming evidence for the beginning to the universe, as we've already discussed, pantheism is false). We are left with theism. As I outlined in earlier exchanges, based upon the historical evidence for the claims of Christ to be God, his proving his claims in history, his authorizing of the Old Testament (which, by the way, he proved to be true because he alone fulfilled all the Old Testament prophecies about himself), and his promising and authorizing of the New Testament, Christianity proves to be the only true theistic religion.

Regarding your question about God's loneliness: The Christian doctrine of the Trinity, which is supported in the Old and New Testaments as earlier discussed, basically states that God is three persons in one divine essence. This is not a contradiction, but it is a paradox. The point here is that in the Trinity, we have a complete community. In fact, we have unity within community, and for this reason God can never be lonely, for he is in perpetual community by his very nature. Because there is community in the first cause, there is community in the effect, that is, in the world he created.

The Trinity also explains the reality and existence of true love. If God were not triune in nature, then how can he be a God of love? Who was he loving? The Trinity explains how and why God is a God of love. There has always been love between the Three Persons of the Trinity, and since there has always been love in the first cause, there is love in the effect (the world he created). Moreover, let's just say he was lonely for argument's sake. If God, an infinite Being, were lonely, then his loneliness would be infinite, and it could not be satisfied by creating finite beings like us. So, it makes no sense for him to create us to overcome a supposed loneliness. Rather, as he reveals in his word and as we see from the intricately designed and finely tuned nature of the universe, God, who in his very nature and being is love, created out of great love for us so that we might be blessed with the experience of knowing life, love, and relationship with him, the infinite, perfect Being. What a blessing and honor that is. We were created so that we might experience him.

Lastly, as discussed in the previous exchange, it simply is not true that there are many paths to God. I know this may be hard to hear and to accept, because it contradicts the popular notion today. We constantly hear that all religions are one, are equally true. However, this is religious relativism, and it is self-defeating in the same way relative notions of truth are self-defeating. It is often said that all religions are superficially different but fundamentally the same. However, any cursory study of world religions reveals that, in fact, all religions are only superficially similar while being fundamentally different. For example, it is true that the major religions do teach similar things about morality, and this makes sense because morality, like truth, is absolute, and God's laws are written on each of our hearts. So, it is not surprising for all cultures to have similar moral codes (they may achieve or express the morality differently, but the underlying moral codes are the same). However, religions do not teach the same things about such fundamental concepts as reality, origins, truth, God, life, death, salvation, and destiny. In fact, the various religions teach opposing views on these key issues, and as we already know, opposites cannot be equally true at the same time in the same way (remember the law of non-contradiction).

So, all religions are not basically the same and thus there cannot be many paths to God. Indeed, there are many paths, but they all do not lead to God. Only one does. Christ said there is only one way to God—through the Son, Jesus Christ (John 14:6). He is either wrong (in which case we are most aggrieved and devoid of hope), or he is right (and as discussed in previous exchanges, the evidence clearly supports the view that he is right). And, as stated in my previous exchange, to claim that there is more than one way to God makes a mockery of Christ and his teachings, and it makes a mockery of the pain, suffering, and sacrifice he endured for us. Faith in the miraculous birth, exemplary life, sacrificial death, and triumphant resurrection of Christ is God's plan, and it was so from the very beginning. It does not involve other paths—only this one (faith in Christ).

We must come back to the point that ideas have consequences, and it does matter what we believe. Of course, we are free to believe what we choose to believe, and I am not going to force you or anyone else to believe one thing or another. But, we must remember that there are consequences to our choices. We must be sure beyond a shadow of doubt that what we believe is in fact the truth. You should be less concerned about how your belief makes you feel. Rather, you should consider if what you believe is true. Are you absolutely sure that you are right? Would you bet your life on it? In the end, that is exactly the wager.

Cheers,
Prof. Dave

Exchange 21

I Have So Much to Think about—What Do I Do Now?

Dear Prof,

Your final question in your last e-mail has really shaken me up a bit. I guess that's a good thing, but I'm not really sure. I've never thought about betting my life on the truthfulness of what I believe. That's a lot to grapple with, and I must admit that a part of me was rather angry at you for even asking that question. I thought maybe you were trying to manipulate me emotionally. Then I reflected over our exchanges, and I realized that, well, you've never really tried to trip me up with emotional appeals in the past, so why would you start now? So, I'm not mad at you (I don't think), but I am unnerved. What does this mean? I don't know. I guess the cry of my heart is that I want to be sure. I keep hearing in my science and philosophy classes that everything is uncertain. But then I think about how you are often turning ideas on their heads, and I realize that these uncertainty advocates seem rather certain that everything is uncertain. (Hey! I think I've learned something from our exchanges.) Your final life wager question is really forcing me to question the livability of total uncertainty. I don't think I can live a lifetime of uncertainty. Deep in my heart, I want to be sure of something. You seem so confident in your faith in Christ. I think there is something to your faith that I want to explore further. Ultimately, I'd like to have assurance in my life. What do I do next?

Sincerely,
Seeker

Dear Seeker,

My heart is indeed full right now. I am so thankful to God for this e-mail you have sent me. Please know that it has been my distinct honor to share these thoughts and truths with you, but please also know that all I have done is given you specific information in as reasonable a manner as I can. Anything else that may be going on in your heart and mind has nothing to do with me. That is between you and God. I am thankful that I have been able to serve you these past several months. I firmly believe that the Hounds of Heaven are nipping at your heels. We may talk in terms of our seeking God, but really, God is seeking and reaching out to us. I believe that you have come to a place in your life where you are questioning origin, purpose, meaning, and destiny. You are seeking real answers to the real questions of how did you get here, why are you here, and where are you going. I am convinced that biblical Christianity holds the true answers to these questions, as we've been discussing all this time. You are basically at a spiritual crossroads, and you need to choose where to go next. You have plenty of information to satisfy the intellect—what you are really facing now is an issue of moral choice or the will. What will you choose?

I am more than happy to continue our discussions, in any manner you feel comfortable, be it through e-mail or in person. However, I want you to consider the following points.

1. **Who is God?** As we've discussed, God is the uncreated, eternal, always existent Creator. He is the uncaused, causal agent who brought all things that are created into being. That is, he created this universe in all of its expansiveness and complexity, he created time itself, he created life, and he has created us in his image to experience his love, to be in fellowship with him and each other, and to worship and honor him. That is our ultimate purpose. And, it is God who determines reality, truth, morality, meaning, and purpose. It is important for us to know and believe this.

2. **Who are we?** We are God's creatures. He created us in his image; we did not create him in our image. He created us to exist in a world in which there is true love that requires true freedom. We have minds and wills and the ability to make true moral choices, which means we are free to choose him or to reject him. In one way or another, we have all chosen to reject him because of our sin nature. Most people will reject this notion of our sin nature. Curiously, the idea that hu-

mans are sinful is the most vehemently rejected concept of our age, yet it is the most empirically verifiable. Do you know any human being who is truly, fully, 100 percent good? Neither do I (other than Jesus Christ—more on that later). Everyone has sinned, and there is no one who is fully good. Only God is sinless. God is the ultimate standard. The question is not how good are you but, rather, are you equally as good as God? In ourselves, we are not good enough to compare with God and, thus, we are not good enough on our own merit to be in God's holy and pure presence.

3. **What do we deserve?** Since we are basically rebels against God, since we all have sinned against the purity of God, since we have all broken God's moral law in one way or another, can we really claim to be worthy to stand in God's holy presence? We deserve to be banished from God's presence because of our sin. This is not because God is a cruel tyrant; rather, it is evidence of his divine justice. What we all deserve is banishment, which is also known as hell. If being in the presence of a holy God is heaven, then banishment because of our rebellion or sin is hell. Note that hell is not a realm of torture that God forces people into; rather, hell is a realm of torment in which we willingly place ourselves by our own rejection of God. God does not desire anyone to be in hell, but we willingly place ourselves there.

4. **What is the solution to our self-imposed banishment?** Because of our rebellion against God, we banish ourselves, and we can do nothing to resolve our broken relationship with God. We broke that relationship and we are not able to fix it ourselves. All the good works in the world will not fix the problem, because any good that we do cannot undo the evil that we have done, nor erase the existence and consequence of sin in our lives. The presence of that sin in our lives disqualifies us from being in God's holy presence. What can we do? Nothing.

Ah, but our helplessness does not mean that nothing can be done. We can do nothing, but God can do anything, and he can save us from our self-imposed banishment. God has saved us through the person of Jesus Christ. Through Christ, the Son, God has expressed his love and mercy while also satisfying the requirements of justice. Christ, God in human form, took the punishment of our sins upon himself, served as the substitutionary sacrifice (meaning he died for our sins and paid our penalty that is justly due us), and has thus redeemed us from the penalty of hell or self-imposed banishment from God. We did not deserve this gift, but God out of mercy and love showed this grace to us. Grace is an undeserved gift, and that is exactly what Christ did for us—though we did not deserve it, he died in our place so that we might not be banished from God. But, more than merely dying, Christ also rose from the dead, thus triumphing over death, proving he is God, and providing eternal life (review the exchanges in which I provided the historical evidences for the resurrection of Christ).

5. **What are we to do with this historical information?** We can accept this by faith or reject it. If we reject this truth, then we condemn ourselves to eternal banishment or hell. Again, it is a banishment of our own doing. However, if we accept this truth on faith, then our broken relationship with God is restored. (Remember, all people live by faith—the question is, in what are you placing your faith? Remember, also, that this is not a simple-minded, blind faith. As our exchanges demonstrate, there is a wealth of logical, empirical, and historical evidences to sustain a rational faith in Christ and his claims.) If we accept God's truth by faith, then we are saved from eternal banishment (hell) and can rest assured in the promises of eternal community with God (heaven).

6. **How do we know if our faith and decision are real?** If you truly accept Jesus Christ by faith as your personal savior, then you will have a change of mind and heart. Gradually, the old self will die and you will experience the birth and development of the new self in Christ. You will desire to love and serve Christ. You will desire to please him. You will desire to follow his moral commands. You will desire to change how you live, act, think, relate to people, and relate to God. You will desire to know God more and more in truth (that is, to know him as he has revealed himself in the Bible). Does this mean your life will be all fun and games? No. Life in this fallen world will be tough. But, you will know the blessings of God's grace in your life. He will walk with you in all things, and he will never leave you. You will experience a life of true joy and abiding peace. Even in the trials, heartaches, and hardships of life (they will still come), you will know joy unspeakable and a peace that surpasses all understanding.

7. **How do you start this new life?** Begin by honestly confessing to God: tell him you believe he is real and that you are his creation; tell him you know that you have rebelled against him and have rejected him; tell him you understand and believe that you deserve banishment for your rebellion and sin; tell him you know that you can do nothing yourself to fix your broken relationship with him; tell him you believe that only by faith in the exemplary life, sacrificial death, and triumphant resurrection of Jesus Christ can you be reconciled to him; tell him you believe all this to be true and that you accept his gift of salvation through believing in Christ. Then, ask God for his help in changing your life from being a rebel against God to being a follower of God. If you sincerely pray this to God and you truly mean it, then I encourage you to find a good church that believes in the Bible, teaches the Bible, and teaches the centrality of Christ. You will need to find a good church in which to learn more about Christ, to grow in faith, and to be in fellowship with other Christians.

8. **What if you are not ready for such a commitment?** Don't worry. Keep seeking honestly with an open heart and an open mind. Continue to read the Bible (I recommend reading through the Gospels, particularly John and Mark). As you are reading, pray to God each day something like this: "God, if you are real, if Jesus is truly all that he claimed to be, open my mind and heart to understand this and to believe it. Take away my unbelief and reveal yourself to me. Show me the truth." If you are sincerely seeking, then I challenge you to do this. I'm confident that God will show you the truth and will give you the faith to believe.

Thank you so much for allowing me to minister to you in this way. You have been honest, sincere, and open. You have asked some really tough questions, and you have been willing to consider the answers given. Believe it or not, you have been a real blessing to me. You have challenged me to dig into my faith, and you have given me an opportunity to serve the Lord Jesus Christ who I profess as my Lord and Savior and whom I love more than anything on this earth. I praise the Lord for this opportunity, and I pray his richest blessings of truth, understanding, and faith in your life.

May God bless you!
Prof. Dave

Bibliography

Copan, Paul. *"That's Just Your Interpretation": Responding to Skeptics Who Challenge Your Faith.* Grand Rapids: Baker, 2001.

———. *"True for You, but Not for Me": Deflating the Slogans that Leave Christians Speechless.* Minneapolis: Bethany House, 1998.

Darwin, Charles. *The Origins of Species by Means of Natural Selection, or the Preservation of Favoured Races in the Struggle for Life.* 1859. New York: Mentor, 1958.

Fowler, Thomas B., and Daniel Keubler. *The Evolution Controversy: A Survey of Competing Theories.* Grand Rapids: Baker, 2007.

Geisler, Norman L. *Chosen but Free: A Balanced View of Divine Election.* 2nd ed. Minneapolis: Bethany House, 2001.

———. *Christian Apologetics.* Grand Rapids: Baker, 1976.

———. *Miracles and the Modern Mind.* Grand Rapids: Baker, 1992.

Geisler, Normal L., and Frank Turek. *I Don't Have Enough Faith to Be an Atheist.* Wheaton, IL: Crossway, 2004.

Geisler, Norman L., and Peter Bocchino. *Unshakable Foundations: Contemporary Answers to Crucial Questions about the Christian Faith.* Minneapolis: Bethany, 2001.

Gonzalez, Guillermo, and Jay Richards. *The Privileged Planet: How Our Place in the Cosmos Is Designed for Discovery.* Washington, DC: Regnery, 2004.

Gould, Stephen J. *Dinosaur in a Haystack.* New York: Harmony, 1995.

———. "Is a New and General Theory of Evolution Emerging?" *Paleobiology* 6 (1980): 119–30.

———. *The Structure of Evolutionary Theory.* Cambridge, MA: Belknap, 2002.

Hunter, Cornelius G. *Science's Blind Spot: The Unseen Religion of Scientific Naturalism.* Grand Rapids: Brazos, 2007.

Lewis, C. S. *Mere Christianity.* 1952. New York: HarperCollins, 2001.

———. *Miracles.* New York: Macmillan, 1960.

Miller, Walter M., Jr. *A Canticle for Leibowitz.* 1959. New York: Bantam, 1997.

Moreland, J. P., ed. *The Creation Hypothesis: Scientific Evidence for an Intelligent Designer.* Downers Grove, IL: InterVarsity, 1994.

Morris, Henry M. *The Genesis Record: A Scientific and Devotional Commentary on the Book of Beginnings.* Grand Rapids: Baker, 1987.

Nash, Ronald H. *Reason and Faith.* Grand Rapids: Zondervan, 1994.

Ross, Hugh. *A Matter of Days: Resolving a Creation Controversy.* Colorado Springs: NavPress, 2004.

Sarfati, Jonathan. *Refuting Compromise: A Biblical and Scientific Refutation of "Progressive Creationism" (Billions of Years) as Popularized by Astronomer Hugh Ross.* Powder Springs, GA: Creation Book, 2004.

Sproul, R. C. *Chosen by God.* Wheaton: Tyndale House, 1986.

Stott, John R. W. *The Cross of Christ.* Downers Grove, IL: InterVarsity, 1986.

Wallace, Daniel B. "The Gospel According to Bart." No pages. Online: http://bible.org/article/gospel-according-bart.

Zacharias, Ravi. *Can Man Live without God?* Dallas: Word, 1994.

Selected Apologetics Resource List

Albright, William F. *The Archaeology of Palestine*. New York: Penguin, 1949.
———. *Archaeology and the Religion of Israel*. Baltimore: Johns Hopkins University Press, 1953.
Barnett, Paul. *Is the New Testament Reliable?* Downers Grove, IL: InterVarsity, 1986.
———. *Jesus and the Logic of History*. Grand Rapids: Eerdmans, 1997.
Behe, Michael J. *Darwin's Black Box: The Biochemical Challenge to Evolution*. New York: Free Press, 1998.
———, ed. *Science and Evidence for Design in the Universe*. Ft. Collins, CO: Ignatius, 2000.
Biran, Avaraham. "House of David." *Biblical Archaeology Review* (March/April 1994).
Blomberg, Craig. *The Historical Reliability of the Gospels*. Downers Grove, IL: InterVarsity, 1987.
Boyd, Gregory A. *Cynic, Sage, or Son of God?* Grand Rapids: Baker, 1995.
Broom, Neil. *How Blind is the Watchmaker?: Nature's Design and the Limits of Naturalistic Science*. 2nd ed. Downers Grove, IL: InterVarsity, 2001.
Brotzman, Ellis. *Old Testament Textual Criticism*. Grand Rapids: Baker, 1994.
Bruce, F. F. *The Books and Parchments: How We Got Our English Bible*. Old Tappan, NJ: Fleming H. Revell, 1984.
———. *The Canon of Scripture*. Downers Grove, IL: InterVarsity, 1988.
———. *Jesus and Christian Origins outside the New Testament*. Grand Rapids: Eerdmans, 1974.
———. *The New Testament Documents: Are They Reliable?* Grand Rapids: Eerdmans, 2003.
Carson, D. A. *How Long, O Lord?: Reflections on Suffering Evil*. 2nd ed. Grand Rapids: Baker Academic, 2006.
Copan, Paul. *"That's Just Your Interpretation": Responding to Skeptics Who Challenge Your Faith*. Grand Rapids: Baker, 2001.
———. *"True for You, but Not for Me": Deflating the Slogans that Leave Christians Speechless*. Minneapolis: Bethany House, 1998.
Craig, William Lane. *Reasonable Faith: Christian Truth and Apologetics*. Wheaton, IL: Crossway, 1994.
———. *The Son Rises: The Historical Evidence for the Resurrection of Jesus*. Eugene, OR: Wipf & Stock, 2001.
———. "The Ultimate Question of Origins: God and the Beginning of the Universe." *Leadership U*. www.leadershipu.com, 2002. http://www.leaderu.com/offices/billcraig/docs/ultimatequestion.html.
Craig, William Lane, and Quentin Smith. *Theism, Atheism and Big Bang Cosmology*. Oxford: Oxford University Press, 1993.

Dembski, William A. *The Design Revolution: Answering the Toughest Questions about Intelligent Design*. Downers Grove, IL: InterVarsity, 2004.

———. *Intelligent Design: The Bridge between Science and Theology*. Downers Grove, IL: InterVarsity, 2002.

———, ed. *Uncommon Dissent: Intellectuals Who Find Darwinism Unconvincing*. Wilmington: ISI, 2004.

Dembski, William A., and James Kushiner, eds. *Signs of Intelligence: Understanding Intelligent Design*. Grand Rapids: Brazos, 2001.

Does God Exist?: William Lane Craig and Anthony Flew Debate. DVD. Norcross, GA: Ravi Zacharias International Ministries, 1998.

Ewert, David. *From Ancient Tablets to Modern Translations: A General Introduction to the Bible*. Grand Rapids: Zondervan, 1983.

Fowler, Thomas B., and Daniel Kueber. *The Evolution Controversy: A Survey of Competing Theories*. Grand Rapids: Baker, 2007.

France, R. T. *The Evidence for Jesus*. Downers Grove, IL: InterVarsity, 1986.

Geisler, Norman L. *Baker Encyclopedia of Christian Apologetics*. Grand Rapids: Baker, 1999.

———. *Christian Apologetics*. Grand Rapids: Baker, 1976.

———. *Miracles and the Modern Mind*. Grand Rapids: Baker, 1992.

Geisler, Norman, and Frank Turek, *I Don't Have Enough Faith to Be an Atheist*. Wheaton, IL: Crossway, 2004.

Geisler, Norman L., and Peter Bocchino. *Unshakable Foundations: Contemporary Answers to Crucial Questions about the Christian Faith*. Minneapolis: Bethany, 2001.

Geisler, Norman L., and Ronald M. Brooks. *When Skeptics Ask*. Wheaton, IL: Victor, 1990.

Geisler, Norman, and William E. Nix. *A General Introduction to the Bible*. Chicago: Moody, 1986.

Geivett, Douglas, and Gary R. Habermas. *Defense of Miracles*. Downers Grove, IL: InterVarsity, 1997.

Gonzales, Guillermo, and Jay Richards. *The Privileged Planet: How Our Place in the Cosmos Is Designed for Discovery*. Washington, DC: Regnery, 2004.

Guinness, Os. *The Call: Finding and Fulfilling the Central Purpose of Your Life*. Nashville: W Publishing Group, 2003.

———. *Unspeakable: Facing Up to the Challenge of Evil*. New York: HarperOne, 2006.

Habermas, Gary. *The Case for the Resurrection of Jesus*. Grand Rapids: Kregel, 2004.

———. *The Historical Jesus: Ancient Evidence for the Life of Christ*. Joplin, MO: College Press, 1996.

Horn, Siegfried H. "Recent Illumination of the Old Testament." *Christianity Today* 12 (1968): 13–17.

Hunter, Cornelius G. *Darwin's God: Evolution and the Problem of Evil*. Grand Rapids: Brazos, 2002.

———. *Darwin's Proof: The Triumph of Religion over Science*. Grand Rapids: Brazos, 2003.

———. *Science's Blind Spot: The Unseen Religion of Scientific Naturalism*. Grand Rapids: Brazos, 2007.

Jastrow, Robert. *God and the Astronomers*. 2nd ed. New York: Norton, 1992.

Johnson, Phillip. *Darwin on Trial*. 2nd ed. Downers Grove, IL: InterVarsity, 1993.

Selected Apologetics Resource List

Kenyon, Fredric. *Our Bible and the Ancient Manuscripts.* New York: Harper & Row, 1958.
Kitchen, K. A. *Ancient Orient and the Old Testament.* Downers Grove, IL: InterVarsity, 1966.
Kreeft, Peter. *Christianity for Modern Pagans.* San Francisco: Ignatius, 1993.
———. *Making Sense Out of Suffering.* Ann Arbor: Servant Books, 1986.
Kreeft, Peter, and Ronald Tacelli. *Handbook of Christian Apologetics.* Downers Grove, IL: InterVarsity, 1994.
Lewis, C. S. *Christian Reflections.* Ed. Walter Hoop. Grand Rapids: Eerdmans, 1967.
———. *Mere Christianity.* 1952. New York: HarperCollins, 2001.
———. *Miracles.* New York: Macmillan, 1960.
McDowell, Josh. *The New Evidence that Demands a Verdict.* Nashville: Thomas Nelson, 1999.
Metzger, Bruce M. *The Text of the New Testament.* New York: Oxford UP, 1968.
Meyer, Stephen C. *Signature in the Cell: DNA and the Evidence for Intelligent Design.* New York: HarperOne, 2009.
Moreland, J. P. *Scaling the Secular City: A Defense of Christianity.* Grand Rapids: Baker, 1987.
Moreland, J. P., and Kai Nielsen. *Does God Exist?* Amherst, NY: Prometheus, 1993.
Morris, Thomas V. *God and the Philosophers: The Reconciliation of Faith and Reason.* Oxford: Oxford University Press, 1996.
Nash, Ronald H. *Reason and Faith.* Grand Rapids: Zondervan, 1994.
Packer, J. I. *Evangelism and the Sovereignty of God.* Downers Grove, IL: InterVarsity, 1991.
———. *Knowing God.* Downers Grove, IL: InterVarsity, 1993.
Piper, John. *Desiring God: Meditations of a Christian Hedonist.* Colorado Springs: Multnomah, 2003.
Simmons, Geoffrey. *What Darwin Didn't Know: A Doctor Dissects the Theory of Evolution.* Eugene, OR: Harvest House, 2004.
Sproul, R. C. *The Consequences of Ideas: Understanding the Concepts that Shaped Our World.* Wheaton, IL: Crossway, 2000.
———. *Essential Truths of the Christian Faith.* Carol Stream, IL: Tyndale House, 1993.
———. *The Holiness of God.* 2nd ed. Carol Stream, IL: Tyndale House, 1998.
Stott, John R. W. *The Cross of Christ.* Downers Grove, IL: InterVarsity, 1986.
Strobel, Lee. *The Case for a Creator.* Grand Rapids: Zondervan, 2004.
Tozer, A. W. *The Knowledge of the Holy: The Attributes of God.* New York: HarperCollins, 1978.
Wells, Jonathan. *Icons of Evolution: Science or Myth? Why Much of What We Teach about Evolution Is Wrong.* Washington, DC: Regnery, 2002.
What Is the Evidence for/against the Existence of God? Debate between William Lane Craig and Peter W. Atkins. DVD. Norcross, GA: Ravi Zacharias International Ministries, 1998.
Wilson, Clifford A. *Rocks, Relics, and Biblical Reliability.* Grand Rapids: Zondervan, 1977.
Wilson, Robert Dick. *A Scientific Investigation of the Old Testament.* Chicago: Moody, 1959.
Wiseman, Donald F. "Archaeological Confirmation of the Old Testament." In *Revelation and the Bible,* ed. Carl Henry, 301–16. Grand Rapids: Baker, 1958.

Yamauchi, Edwin. *The Stones and the Scriptures*. Philadelphia: Lippincott, 1972.
Zacharias, Ravi. *Can Man Live without God?* Dallas: Word, 1994.
———. *Has Christianity Failed You?* Grand Rapids: Zondervan, 2010.
———. *The Real Face of Atheism*. Grand Rapids: Baker, 2004.
Zacharias, Ravi, and Norman Geisler, eds. *Who Made God? And Answers to over 100 Other Tough Questions of Faith*. Grand Rapids: Zondervan, 2003.

www.ingramcontent.com/pod-product-compliance
Lightning Source LLC
Chambersburg PA
CBHW050845160426
43192CB00011B/2157